home at 7 dinner at 8

Sophie Wright

home at 7
dinner at 8

Sophie Wright

Photography by
RomaS Foord

KYLE BOOKS

Dedication

I would like to dedicate this book to my Mom. Thanks for everything Mom. I love you very much.

Published in 2012 by Kyle Books
www.kylebooks.com

Distributed by National Book Network
4501 Forbes Blvd., Suite 200
Lanham, MD 20706
Phone: (800) 462-6420
Fax: (301) 429-5746
custserv@nbnbooks.com

First Published in Great Britain in 2011 by Kyle Books

ISBN: 978-1-906868-48-2

Text © Sophie Wright 2011
Photographs © Romas Foord 2011
Design © Kyle Cathie Limited 2011

Editor: Vicky Orchard
Design: Nicky Collings
Photography: Romas Foord
Styling: Polly Webb-Wilson
Copy editor: Emma Callery
Production: Sheila Smith and Nic Jones

Library of Congress Control Number: 2011941331

Color reproduction by Altaimage Ltd
Printed and bound in China by Toppan Leefung Printing Ltd

Note on ingredients
All eggs are large unless otherwise stated.

Acknowledgments

This book has been an absolute pleasure to write, and since we came up with idea around the table in the Kyle Cathie office, I've not been able to stop thinking of fun, quick, and easy recipes that would suit the title of this fabulous book. It's a book for all people from all walks of life, but I must admit that I kept a few very key people in mind while writing it (Carly, Rosie, Tom...).

My main aim with *Home at 7, Dinner at 8* was accessibility. I want this book to be a bible of yummy recipes that everyone can have a go at. And yes Hannah, I'm talking about YOU! Hannah, you are my working girl stencil for making this book work! Mainly because if you can do it...anyone can!! So thank you for always giving it a go, and for letting me watch you make potato custard soup. Definitely an experience. Dan, you know what I'm talking about!!

I really want to mention my Mom, Ann, who is such a special person. You have not only given me my passion for food and cooking but also the ability to put my mind to something and do it well.

A lot has changed in my life over the last year or so, and I can say that this has probably been the best year yet. I have had the praise, support, and kindness from people that will be with me forever. Tom...of course no meal is complete without a touch of Pepper!! You have been a tower of strength to me, not just with the book, but with everything, and I hope someday I can be as strong for you as you have been for me.

Oliver Wright, my beautiful little brother…Olly, I hope one day, when you're old enough to read this that you learn something and don't just open a can! I promise I'll always lend you a hand if you ever get stuck.

Dad, not much else I can say other than you're not only an amazing father to me but also to Oliver, and you're my absolute role model. I'm very proud to be your daughter.

Finally, I must give a huge thanks to everyone at Kyle Cathie who has allowed this book to happen: Vicky, you're a star of an editor, and your patience and attention to detail must certainly be praised. Thank you for all your hard work. Nicky, genius as ever, you are an absolute pleasure. And Romas, I must say that every shoot day was fabulous and you made making this book such an enjoyable experience. The pictures are stunning! Well done all of you—I hope you all love it as much as I do.

I know there are so many of you I have left out, but as with *Easy Peasy*, all my lovely friends and family—I want to thank you so much. I'm extremely lucky to have you all and hope you enjoy reading my new book that I have loved writing so much.

MAKE LIFE EASY FOR YOURSELF

Being able to cook a simple dinner that is ready to eat within an hour of getting home is something that everyone craves. But sometimes cooking a meal after a long day at work can seem like a tedious task. For me cooking should be enjoyable—a way of winding down at the end of the day, perhaps with a glass of wine and a bit of music, or chatting to a friend or partner about your day while making a delicious meal. Easy, tasty, and fresh dishes that can be prepared quickly with little effort and without sacrificing on flavor.

This book has the answer: all recipes can be on the table in an hour or less (most in 30 minutes and under), are suitable for a variety of occasions, and can be enjoyed by friends, family, adults, and children alike. I want this book to be the hardworking professional's bible that you can scan through the night before and know what you're going to pick up from the grocery store on your way home. I'll introduce you to a few of my favorite time-saving cheats, just to take the strain off, give you some suggestions for pantry essentials, the basics you'll use over and over, and show you how by having a few items of the right equipment you can become so much more confident when it comes to cooking. I also plan on showing you, in Watching Your Pennies, how you can make really great family dinners without breaking the bank. So many ingredients are available for us in the supermarket that we often walk straight past the real bargains. I aim to help you open your eyes a bit.

I always tended to go for the more difficult option when cooking (no shortcuts). That's fine on the weekends when you might have time to spare, but honestly, who does during the week? I now know that it's absolutely fine to use a few things such as preprepared ingredients that make your life much easier in the long run and make cooking far less stressful and time-consuming.

I really want to stress that cooking isn't about getting worried that you are missing a certain ingredient or you can't find what you need in the store. Go with what you've got and take it easy. The minute you start to get stressed, the less enjoyable and relaxing your cooking time will be. Just have fun.

When cooking during the week, I've now changed my whole attitude. I do whatever I can think of that's tasty and can be cooked in quick time. I want the opportunity to enjoy relaxing or spending time with my friends or family, not be dragged away from them by the cooking while they are unwinding in front of the TV with a glass of something cold.

I know it's easy to order takeout, or walk down to your local restaurant for a bite to eat, but I hope these recipes will not only make your mouth water but will also inspire you to cook at home and enjoy a quicker, healthier, and money-saving alternative. I have written this book to encourage you all that cooking something interesting and fast in an evening can be done—and with new, exciting recipes. Enjoy!

ESSENTIAL INGREDIENTS

These are just a handful of things that we can buy to make our lives so much easier when cooking during the week.

PANTRY

Fresh ready-made gnocchi, tortellini, and ravioli—enable you to eat meals that would otherwise take hours to make, without sacrificing quality

Any type of dry or fresh pasta such as spaghetti, penne, or fusilli

Instant Asian noodles such as cellophane noodles, ready-cooked, soba, or instant noodles

Ready-cooked microwavable rice—helps you save on cooking and cleanup

Ready-cooked lentils, either canned or packaged—save 20 to 25 minutes by buying ready-cooked lentils and lose none of the nutritional benefits

Infused oils such as chili, basil, lemon, garlic, avocado, or nut oils—add instant flavor to any dish

Vinegars: balsamic (reasonable quality), hard cider, white wine, red wine, rice wine—allow you to be far more creative in the kitchen and bring out real flavor in foods you might otherwise avoid

Ready-made stocks and bouillon cubes—a pantry must-have no kitchen can be without. You can also bulk freeze premade stocks to use when necessary

Dried herbs such as dried oregano, thyme, herbes de Provence

Spices and premixed spice blends such as ground cumin, ground coriander, *ras el hanout*, garam masala—instantly jazz up a piece of fish, roasted veggies, or chicken breast

Dried red pepper flakes—use these when you don't have fresh chiles to add a little spice to a dish

Good-quality pestos and pastes—available from the chilled food section of the grocery store and keep a good week or so in the fridge

Sweet chili sauce

Soy sauce—light and dark

Canned and strained tomatoes and paste—inexpensive, never spoil, and an occasional life-saver for a quick pasta dish when supplies are low

Marinated artichokes in a jar or fresh from the deli section—a great ingredient to have when you feel like being a bit more creative

Semi-dried tomatoes or jar of sun-dried (the best quality are available from the fresh deli section)—full of flavor, as someone else has done all the hard work of preparing them for you

Jar of ready-roasted bell peppers and vegetables

Prepicked pomegranate seeds—colorful and healthy, they add a bit of punch to any exotic dish

Canned beans such as cannellini beans, kidney beans, flageolet beans, borlotti beans, lima beans, and chickpeas (garbanzo beans)—saves the fuss of soaking them in water and provide a good source of inexpensive protein and a way of bulking out dinners

Ready-chopped garlic, ginger, and chiles

FRIDGE

Parmesan, cheddar, or Gruyère and any type of blue cheese

Cream cheese

Eggs—handy for a quick omelet or fritters

Lemons

Onions

Small selection of fresh herbs if possible

FREEZER

Berries such as mixed fruits, strawberries, blackberries, raspberries

Peas

Fava and soybeans

Spinach

Lots of ice—handy for making drinks

Bay leaves, thyme, and fresh chiles—keep really well in the freezer

Preprepared stocks—either store-bought or homemade

Shrimp

EQUIPMENT AND COOKING TECHNIQUES

Now that you have a nicely stocked kitchen I'm going to let you in on a few little secrets on how to prepare all these great dinners you are going to cook with ease. Cooking isn't rocket science. It's all about common sense. What would you think if I tried to cook a nice piece of fish in an old beaten-up pan or chop parsley with a blunt knife? Trust me; I see this time and time again while doing my rounds of cooking lessons.

Here's a list of a few things I think you must have in order to be able to get home at 7 and have dinner at 8. Some of you may read this little list and say, well, I've got all that. If that's the case, then just skip this section. If not, get a pen and paper and start writing that shopping list!

A sharp knife Not a knife that is so big you can't use it, just a simple 12-inch chef's knife that can be used for almost every task.

A small serrated knife These are great for preparing ingredients like cherry tomatoes and citrus fruits. I couldn't be without mine.

A blender of sorts I know many of you will have a big old chunky blender hanging around at the back of a kitchen cabinet that hasn't seen the light of day since it came out the box, so I would advise getting yourself a space-saving option that fits in even the smallest of drawers and gets used on a regular basis. These compact blenders cost a maximum of $40 and trust me they are worth every cent. I use mine for everything from chopping chiles and garlic for curries to making a quick fresh pesto.

A good-quality nonstick pan. This will make all the difference when cooking even the simplest of meals. They are great for pan-frying fish, chicken breasts, and eggs and making quick stir-fries if you don't have a wok. A nonstick pan is also a healthier option, as you only need use half the amount of oil when cooking because nothing will stick to it.

Sharp scissors Seems obvious, but scissors are great when it comes to time-saving for everything from quickly snipping herbs through removing the backbone from a chicken.

A fine grater There are many different options on the market for sharp, fine graters and they are brilliant for everything from grating Parmesan, garlic, and ginger to zesting lemons.

A casserole pan with a lid A kitchen must-have.

I think if you have these few basic tools, your whole view on cooking will change. These are really easy solutions to making your life just that little bit easier.

Finally, a few handy tips when it comes to cooking:

Before you start cooking a recipe, familiarize yourself with it. You don't have to learn it by heart but just get a vague idea of the steps and what's meant to be going on and when. This way you won't need to have your head buried in a book while slightly overcooking the onions! You'll also feel so much more confident with the idea of cooking it.

Prepare all the ingredients before you actually start cooking anything. This means any chopping or blending that needs to be done should be completed before you even turn on the heat under a pan. Do this while your oven or broiler is preheating. I promise this will save you time in the long run.

Don't overstretch yourself when cooking for friends or family so you end up getting stressed out. Cooking should be a nice, relaxing experience wherever possible and also inventive. If something goes wrong, don't panic, it's probably still edible. None of us are perfect. If something goes wrong or doesn't taste right, one of the following tricks might help:

Fresh herbs liven up even the blandest of dishes, so try to keep a small variety in your fridge and use them whenever you can.

If you're using chiles and you've gotten carried away, try adding a squeeze of lemon or a spoonful of yogurt or heavy cream. That will usually calm down the spice a bit.

Never cook green vegetables with a lid on the saucepan, and make sure the water is rapidly boiling before you add them so you don't overcook and waterlog your vegetables.

Lastly, I have experienced what I'm sure many of you struggle with—a small kitchen! So I understand how difficult it can be cooking for any more than two people in a limited space. I've really made the effort to take this into account when designing these recipes; I've tried to use as few pots and pans as possible and hopefully most of the dishes can go in the dishwasher. If you don't have one, then leave washing the dishes for someone else—one of my biggest rules is that if I cook, then there's no way I'm doing cleanup!

Everyday

Most of us after a long day just want dinner on the table (or our knees) as quickly as possible, so your evening can start and you can finally relax. We want food that is quick, simple to prepare, and easy to eat. I have filled this chapter with recipes that will become a tried-and-trusted part of your weekly meal menu. We all have favorites that we cook time and time again because we can virtually prepare them with our eyes closed and that's exactly what I've planned for with these dishes. It's really important to me that these recipes are as accessible as possible and, of course, easy to shop for. Nothing flashy—just good, friendly food.

ROASTED GUINEA FOWL WITH ENDIVE, FENNEL, AND ORANGE

55
___
TOTAL

Preparation 15
Cooking 40
Serves 4

It's always nice to have a change from a roast chicken, and guinea fowl is the closest variation. It's the same-size bird, so cooks in the same amount of time, but it has a meatier flavor than chicken and slightly darker meat. It's best to remove the legs and wings from the crown so it cooks more quickly. It's really delicious with rustic roasted vegetables (I like to buy red endive heads, as they add a bit of color) and a few herbs and spices. Give it a go—you may be surprised.

1 guinea fowl, 3 to 3½ pounds
2 fennel bulbs, trimmed and cut into thin slices
3 to 4 heads of red endive, halved lengthwise
4 carrots, peeled and cut into sticks

2 large oranges
2 tablespoons maple syrup
1 tablespoon fennel seed
1 tablespoon chopped thyme leaves
2 tablespoons olive oil
salt and freshly ground black pepper

1 Preheat the oven to 375°F. Remove the legs from the guinea fowl by pulling them away from the carcass and cutting the skin that holds the legs to the body. Pull each leg back on itself and it should pop out of the carcass. Use your knife to cut it away completely. Remove the wings also if you wish.

2 Mix the fennel and endive with the carrots in a big bowl and grate in the zest of both the oranges. Pour over the maple syrup, add the fennel seeds and thyme, and stir everything together thoroughly to coat.

3 Line a roasting pan with wax paper and scatter the vegetables. Lay the pieces of guinea fowl on top, drizzle with olive oil, and season well with salt and pepper. Cut the oranges in half and put these in the pan as well. They get very juicy as they heat up and will be the dressing for the guinea fowl. Roast in the oven for about 40 minutes until everything is cooked through, and the guinea fowl has nice crispy skin.

4 Remove and let rest while you squeeze the oranges over the vegetables and the cooked bird. Carve the crown and serve in pieces, separating the drumsticks from the thighs so everyone gets a bit of leg and a bit of breast.

This recipe also works really well with chicken.

A GREAT BIG SALAD OF ROASTED SQUASH, PANEER, RADICCHIO, AND PROSCIUTTO

35
TOTAL

Preparation 10
Cooking 25
Serves 2
or 4 as a side dish

This recipe can also be made using chicory if you can't find radicchio.

This really is a great throw-in-the-oven kind of dish that requires only a little preparation in terms of chopping and can be eaten hot, warm, or cold. You can have it as your main meal, but I also like it as a side with some roasted fish or maybe a pan-fried pork chop. It's really versatile and full of flavor.

1 butternut squash, skin left on, seeded and cut into large chunks
9 ounces panir or firm tofu, cubed
2 teaspoons honey
salt and freshly ground black pepper
1 teaspoon ground cumin
1 teaspoon dried red pepper flakes

2 red radicchio lettuces, cut into eighths
2 tablespoons olive oil, plus extra to drizzle
2 tablespoons balsamic vinegar
12 to 16 slices prosciutto or Parma ham
juice of 1 lemon
3½ ounces arugula

1 Preheat the oven to 400°F. Line a roasting pan with wax paper and spread out the squash and panir or tofu on it. Pour over the honey and season with salt, pepper, cumin, and the red pepper flakes. Scatter the radicchio over the top. Drizzle the whole pan with the olive oil and balsamic vinegar. Roast for about 25 minutes until the radicchio is slightly charred on the thinner parts of the leaves and the honey is caramelizing a little on the edges of the panir.

2 Remove from the oven and transfer to a serving plate. Tear over the ham. Drizzle over the lemon juice and some extra olive oil, and scatter on the arugula. Make sure you pour over any drippings that might be left in the roasting pan and serve.

STEAMED SEA BREAM WITH GINGER, CHILE, AND SCALLIONS

16
___
TOTAL

Preparation 10
Cooking 6
Serves 2
as a light dinner

This is a really healthy fish dish packed full of flavor and freshness. It helps to have a bamboo steamer to cook this recipe, but don't worry if you haven't got one. An upturned saucer in the bottom of a shallow pan will do the trick as long as your pan has a lid. Striped bass is a nice substitute if you can't find sea bream.

2 fillets of sea bream, pin-boned
2 tablespoons light soy sauce
1 teaspoon sesame oil
½ teaspoon white sugar
1 tablespoon rice vinegar
1¼-inch piece of fresh ginger, peeled and sliced into very thin strips
1 large green pepper, sliced on the angle
6 scallions, trimmed and cut into thin strips (as you would see with Peking duck in a Chinese restaurant)

To serve
a large handful of cilantro
1 lime, cut into wedges
steamed rice or a selection of green vegetables

1 Put a wok or saucepan with a steamer on the stove (or see the recipe introduction, above) and half fill the wok or saucepan with boiling water. Cover with the lid.

2 Lay the fillets of fish, skin-side down, on a plate that fits inside the steamer. Combine the soy sauce, sesame oil, sugar, and vinegar in a bowl. Sprinkle the ginger, chile, and half the scallions over the fish fillets and pour over all the sauce.

3 Put the plate into the steamer and put the lid on tight. Let steam until the fish is cooked through, about 6 minutes.

4 Serve the fish with all the bits on top and tear over the cilantro leaves and remaining scallions. Pour any drippings on the plate over the fish and serve with a wedge of lime and steamed rice or green vegetables.

This dish goes really well with the Pineapple Skewers with Vanilla and Maple Syrup (see page 157).

SPICED LAMB MEATBALLS WITH PUMPKIN, APRICOT, AND TOMATO STEW

55

TOTAL

Preparation 20
Cooking 35
Serves 4 to 6

This is a Moroccan-ish dish that I cook a lot because you can make copious quantities of it, leave it in the fridge, and have it a hundred different ways for the next couple of days, saving you valuable time. I have even been known to make a monster sandwich with the leftover meatballs and sauce.

For the meatballs
18 ounces ground lamb
1 teaspoon ground cumin
1 teaspoon ground coriander
½ teaspoon chili powder
½ bunch of cilantro, finely chopped
4 to 5 sprigs of mint leaves, finely chopped
1 egg yolk
1 teaspoon salt
freshly ground black pepper
2 tablespoons vegetable oil

For the pumpkin, apricot, and tomato stew
2 tablespoons vegetable oil
2 onions, peeled and diced
1 teaspoon ground ginger
2 red peppers, finely chopped

3 garlic cloves, peeled and finely chopped
1 teaspoon ground cumin
1 pumpkin, skin left on, seeded
  and diced
⅔ cup coarsely chopped dried apricots
2 x 14-ounce cans diced tomatoes
¾ cup plus 1 tablespoon chicken or
  vegetable stock

To serve
a small handful of mint leaves,
  finely chopped
Greek-style yogurt
Pomegranate and Almond Couscous,
  see page 43 (optional)

1 To make the meatballs, combine all the ingredients, except for the vegetable oil, really well. Roll into golfball-size balls and leave on a tray in the fridge while you prepare the stew.

2 Heat 2 tablespoons of oil in a large, heavy-bottom pan and add the onion, ground ginger, chiles, and garlic. Cook until softened, 5 to 6 minutes, then add the ground cumin and cook well. Add the pumpkin, apricots, canned tomatoes, and the stock and bring to a boil, then reduce the heat and let simmer for 20 minutes.

3 Meanwhile, heat a large skillet and 2 tablespoons of vegetable oil. Remove the meatballs from the fridge and pan-fry in the hot oil until nicely browned on all sides, about 5 minutes. Transfer them to the stew using a slotted spoon.

4 Cook for an additional 5 minutes before serving with a scattering of fresh mint, a dollop of Greek-style yogurt, and the Pomegranate and Almond Couscous, if you like.

As well as the
suggested
couscous, this
recipe is also
very good stirred
through pasta.

BRAISED SAUSAGE WITH GORGONZOLA POLENTA

40

TOTAL

Preparation 10
Cooking 30
Serves 4

This is comfort food at its best. It's basically sausage and mashed potatoes but without the mashing. Polenta is a really underused ingredient because a lot of people don't really know what to do with it. It's great because it's so simple to prepare and a little goes a long way. Polenta needs to be flavored since it can be a bit bland and Gorgonzola is perfect, as the creamy blue cheese melts easily into the wet polenta. If you are not a blue cheese fan, use Taleggio instead.

8 good-quality meaty sausages
3 red onions, peeled and sliced
3 garlic cloves, peeled and chopped or
 1½ teaspoons ready-chopped garlic
a small pinch of dried red pepper flakes
1 teaspoon herbes de Provence
2 teaspoons tomato paste
salt and freshly ground black pepper
⅔ cup red wine
1 tablespoon balsamic vinegar
1 tablespoon liquid beef broth concentrate
1 teaspoon white sugar

1 cup chicken stock

For the polenta
2 cups plus 1 tablespoon chicken stock
1 cup plus 1 tablespoon lowfat milk
1 teaspoon herbes de Provence
1⅔ cups quick-cook polenta
7 ounces Gorgonzola
4 tablespoons butter

To serve
freshly grated Parmesan cheese

1 Start by heating a medium-size skillet on the stove. Pan-fry the sausage until golden brown on all sides. Remove from the pan and add the onions, garlic, red pepper flakes, and herbes de Provence. Sauté for 5 minutes before adding the tomato paste and stirring well. Season with salt and pepper.

2 Return the sausage to the pan with the onions, pour in the wine, vinegar, beef concentrate broth, sugar, and chicken stock and simmer until the sausages are cooked through, 15 to 20 minutes. If the sauce starts to dry out, add a splash of water.

3 Just before you are ready to serve, make the polenta. Heat the chicken stock in a saucepan with the milk and herbes de Provence. When the mixture starts to boil, beat the liquid quickly and slowly pour in the polenta. The mixture should thicken quite quickly. Season with pepper and beat in the Gorgonzola and butter.

4 Serve the polenta immediately divided among four plates, each topped with two sausages and the sauce they were cooked in. Scatter over some freshly grated Parmesan cheese.

Don't leave the polenta sitting around for too long or it will start to firm up. It needs to be cooked just before you are ready to serve.

ASIAN NOODLE SOUP WITH SHRIMP

20

TOTAL

Preparation 10

Cooking 10

Serves 2

One of the all-time easiest recipes to cook after a long day and, once you've got your pantry stocked with the right Asian items, the shopping for this dinner will be nothing more than some fresh herbs and perhaps a few chiles. It's very versatile and can be made with any vegetables, fish, or meat you like or happen to have in the fridge.

For the stock

2 cups plus 1 tablespoon chicken stock
2 garlic cloves, peeled and sliced or
   1 teaspoon ready-chopped garlic
1 teaspoon dried red pepper flakes
1 tablespoon sweet chili sauce
1 tablespoon dark soy sauce
1 tablespoon oyster sauce
½ teaspoon sesame oil
salt (optional)

For the soup

7 ounces dried soba noodles or instant
   noodles
10 to 12 raw medium shrimp, peeled and
   deveined
2 heads of bok choy, cut into quarters
1 red pepper, sliced
½ bunch of cilantro, chopped
3 scallions, trimmed and cut into slices
1 lime, cut into wedges

1 The key to a good soup is a good stock, so the first job is making the broth big and bold in flavor. Pour the stock into a saucepan and place on high heat. Add the remaining ingredients and let the broth to come to a boil. Taste it to check for the spicy/salty balance. If necessary, add more sweet chili sauce or salt to taste.

2 Add the noodles and the shrimp and cook until the noodles are cooked through, 4 to 5 minutes. Fold the bok choy into the soup and cook until the leaves are tender and the stalk still has a crunch, about 2 to 3 minutes.

3 Serve in deep soup bowls and sprinkle with the sliced chile, ciilantro, and scallions. Serve with a wedge of lime on the side.

Add a can of coconut milk to this soup to give it a Thai feel.

SHREDDED CHICKEN AND TORTELLINI ONE-BOWL WONDER

🕐
15
TOTAL

Preparation 5
Cooking 10
Serves 2

Why not finish off this meal with some Ricotta and Raspberry Fritters (see page 160)?

This dish can be anything you want it to be—a soup, broth, or a stew. Call it what you like, all that matters is that it's quick, tasty, healthy, and hassle-free.

1 quart chicken stock
5½ ounces fresh tortellini with a filling of any flavor
2 big handfuls of fava beans or soybeans (frozen is fine)
1¼ cups shredded cooked chicken (store-bought or leftover)

1 zucchini, cut into ribbons with a peeler
salt and freshly ground black pepper

To serve
a large handful of basil leaves
Parmesan cheese shavings

1 Pour the chicken stock into a saucepan and bring to a boil. Add the tortellini and beans and cook for 3 minutes before adding the shredded chicken and the zucchini ribbons. Cook until the chicken is heated through and then season with lots of salt and pepper.

2 Serve in big soup bowls with freshly torn basil and shaved Parmesan cheese.

ORANGE-MARINATED PORK CHOPS WITH A HAZELNUT AND PARSLEY DRESSING

40

TOTAL

Preparation 20
plus, marinating time

Cooking 20

Serves 4

Pork goes perfectly with most things sweet and slightly acidic, so pork and orange is a brilliant combination. This dish has almost no chopping, so all that really needs to be done after the dressing is made is to throw the meat on a hot grill pan or under a hot broiler and wait for it to be cooked.

For the marinade
zest and juice of 2 large oranges
2 tablespoons honey
4 sprigs of thyme, leaves only
1 tablespoon whole-grain mustard
1 tablespoon sherry vinegar
salt and freshly ground black pepper

For the pork chops
4 pork chops on the bone (try to make sure they have a good layer of fat on them)

For the hazelnut and parsley dressing
scant 1 cup coarsely chopped hazelnuts
1 tablespoon whole-grain mustard
zest and juice of 1 orange
2 teaspoons honey
1 teaspoon sherry vinegar
3 tablespoons olive oil
a large bunch of flatleaf parsley, coarsely chopped
Radicchio and Prosciutto Salad (see page 16), to serve (optional)

1 To make the marinade, combine the orange zest and juice with the honey, thyme, mustard, vinegar, and salt and pepper in a large mixing bowl.

2 Score the fat on the pork chops four or five times to stop the chops curling up too much. Place the chops in the marinade and let stand while you heat up the grill pan or broiler.

3 To make the dressing, toast the hazelnuts in a heated dry skillet for 1 to 2 minutes and then set aside. Mix the mustard with the orange zest and juice, honey, vinegar, and olive oil. Season with salt and pepper.

4 The grill pan or broiler should now be hot enough (a grill pan should be nearly smoking and on the highest heat). Lay the chops on the grill pan or under the broiler and cook until charred in some places (because of the sugar in the marinade), moving them around should stop this from happening too much, 6 to 8 minutes. Brush the chops with the marinade during the cooking time to keep them nice and moist. Turn the chops over and cook for an additional 6 to 8 minutes on the other side. Transfer to a plate and let rest.

Fantastic cooked on the barbecue if the sun is shining.

5 To serve, add the hazelnuts and parsley to the dressing mix. Transfer the chops to individual plates and spoon over the dressing. Serve with the salad on the side.

PAN-ROASTED LAMB WITH CARROT AND FETA SALAD AND RED CURRANT DRESSING

35
TOTAL

Preparation 15
Cooking 20
Serves 4

When I have a salad for my dinner, I want it to be quite substantial and filling, otherwise I'm hungry half an hour later and find myself raiding the cookie jar. I like to have lots of different colors and textures going on and to combine some hot elements with a cold salad.

6 large carrots, peeled and cut into chunky sticks or batons
2 tablespoons honey
2 tablespoons olive oil, plus extra for cooking the lamb
2 teaspoons cumin seed
1 teaspoon ground coriander
salt and freshly ground black pepper
4 lamb tenderloin fillets, weighing about 7 ounces each
1½ cups cubed feta

3 tablespoons coarsely chopped pitted black olives
5½ ounces mixed salad leaves
a small bunch of cilantro
3 tablespoons pumpkin seeds

For the dressing
2 tablespoons red currant jelly
1 tablespoon red wine vinegar
2 tablespoons olive oil
1 teaspoon Dijon mustard

1 Preheat the oven to 400°F. Mix the carrots in a bowl with the honey, olive oil, cumin seed, ground coriander, and salt and pepper.

2 Line a roasting pan with wax paper and lay out the carrots evenly on the pan. Roast in the oven for about 15 to 20 minutes until they are slightly charred around the edges but still have a little bite to them.

3 While the carrots are cooking, heat up a large skillet on the highest setting. Oil the lamb fillets and season with salt and pepper. Lay them in the smoking hot pan and cook for about 5 to 6 minutes on each side, depending on the thickness, until the meat is nicely caramelized on the outside and is slightly firm to the touch. Remove the pan from the heat and let rest.

4 To make the dressing, combine all the ingredients in a small saucepan and bring to a boil, beating to remove any lumps. When combined, turn off the heat and set aside.

5 When the carrots are cooked, remove from the oven and place in a large bowl. Scatter in the feta, black olives, and salad leaves and season with pepper. Slice the lamb and mix into the salad. Tear in the cilantro leaves and mix through before pouring over the red currant dressing. Transfer the salad to a large platter and sprinkle over the pumpkin seeds. Eat straight away before the heat wilts the salad leaves.

The dressing can be made in advance and will keep for a week in the fridge.

PEA AND SALMON FISHCAKES

40

TOTAL

Preparation 25

Cooking 15

Serves 4

The main time-consuming element when making fishcakes is the mash, so I wondered if there was an alternative ingredient that I could use to bind the fish together. Peas are perfect for this and also work really well with the flavors of the other ingredients.

For the fishcakes
1½ cups frozen peas (petits pois are best)
7 ounces smoked salmon trimmings
18 ounces salmon, skinned, pin-boned, and cut into ½-inch pieces
zest of 2 lemons and juice of 1 lemon
a small bunch of dill, coarsely chopped
1 egg
3 scallions, trimmed and chopped
1 tablespoon all-purpose flour
salt and freshly ground black pepper

For the fishcake coating
heaping ¾ cup all-purpose flour
2 eggs, beaten
1½ cups fine dry bread crumbs or heaping 1 cup polenta
4 tablespoons olive oil

For the sauce
1 cup crème fraîche or sour cream
zest and juice of 1 lemon
1 tablespoon whole-grain mustard

14 ounces wilted spinach (optional)

1 Bring a pan of water to a boil with a pinch of salt added. Once boiling, blanch the peas for 20 to 30 seconds before draining and running under cold water to cool. Put the peas into a blender along with all the remaining ingredients for the fishcakes, except for the seasoning, and pulse until the mixture has combined. Season with plenty of salt and pepper.

2 Put the flour, eggs, and bread crumbs or polenta into three separate bowls. Make eight patties out of the fishcake mix and pass first though the flour, then the egg, and finally the bread crumbs or polenta. Put the patties on a baking sheet and let stand in the fridge until you are ready to cook them.

3 When you are ready to eat, preheat the oven to 375°F. Pour the olive oil into a skillet and turn the heat to medium. Lay the fishcakes in the pan (you will probably need to do this in two or three batches) and cook for about 2 to 3 minutes on each side until they are golden brown. Remove the partly cooked fishcakes from the pan, return them to the baking sheet, and bake in the oven for 6 to 8 minutes until cooked through.

4 While they are in the oven, heat up the crème fraîche or sour cream in a small pan with the lemon zest and juice and the whole-grain mustard. Remove the cooked fishcakes from the oven and serve with the sauce and wilted spinach, if you like.

For a quick accompaniment, pierce a bag of spinach a few times and cook in a microwave on high for 3 minutes.

A VERY EASY BAKED RICOTTA PIE

35

TOTAL

Preparation 10

Cooking 25

Serves 4 to 6

as a dinner with a
salad, or 6 to 8 as an
accompaniment

**If you feel like
something a
bit different, try
adding some
fried bacon and
caramelized
onions to the
ricotta before
mixing.**

I'm not entirely sure where I learned this recipe, but I do know that I make it all the time, either as a side dish if I have a few people over for dinner, or as an alternative to an omelet if I feel like something a bit different. Much like an omelet, you can add whatever ingredients you like, but I also like to eat it on its own with a green salad (making sure there is some left over in the fridge for the next day, as it's great cold as well).

2 tablespoons olive oil
2 cups ricotta
2 egg yolks
3 large eggs
1 cup crème fraîche or sour cream

salt and freshly ground black pepper
2 sprigs of thyme, leaves only
2¾ ounces ready-roasted bell peppers,
   sliced into thin strips
½ cup grated Parmesan cheese

1 Preheat the oven to 400°F. Grease a medium-size baking dish with the olive oil. Beat the ricotta and eggs together in a food processor until light and pale in color. (This can also be done using a hand-held electric mixer.)

2 When pale, add the crème fraîche or sour cream and mix in well. Season with a large pinch of salt and plenty of pepper. Stir in the thyme leaves, pour the mixture into the baking dish, and scatter over the sliced bell peppers. Poke them down into the mixture so they won't burn. Sprinkle the Parmesan cheese over the top.

3 Bake in the oven for 20 to 25 minutes. The mixture should be set with a very slight wobble. Let cool for 10 minutes before serving.

PANTRY PASTA

20
TOTAL

Preparation 5
Cooking 15
Serves 4

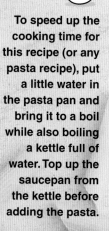

To speed up the cooking time for this recipe (or any pasta recipe), put a little water in the pasta pan and bring it to a boil while also boiling a kettle full of water. Top up the saucepan from the kettle before adding the pasta.

There are some things that we all have in our pantry and I think it's very important to know how to make them into a tasty dinner. Here, I'm talking pasta; for this dish I like to use penne, but any type will do. Very easy to prepare with everything thrown into one pan so there's hardly any dishwashing, it's ideal if you haven't had time to shop.

salt and freshly ground black pepper
18 ounces dried pasta
2 tablespoons olive oil, plus extra to serve
1 red onion, peeled and chopped
2 garlic cloves, peeled and chopped or
   2 teaspoons ready-chopped garlic
1 x 14-ounce can diced tomatoes
½ cup white wine
½ teaspoon dried red pepper flakes

1 teaspoon balsamic vinegar
½ teaspoon white sugar
2 tablespoons capers in vinegar, drained
2 x 7-ounce cans tuna, drained
2 tablespoons pitted black olives

To serve
a small handful of basil leaves (optional)
grated Parmesan cheese (optional)

1 Bring a big pot of water to a boil and add a pinch of salt. When the water starts to boil, add the pasta and cook as directed on the package until al dente.

2 Place a skillet on the stove, add the oil, onion, and garlic and let soften, 4 to 5 minutes. Add the canned tomatoes, white wine, red pepper flakes, vinegar, and sugar. After a few minutes add the capers, tuna, and olives. Season with salt and pepper and let simmer while the pasta cooks.

3 Drain the pasta and mix with the sauce. Serve with the basil leaves and grated Parmesan cheese, if you like, and a drizzle of olive oil.

ROASTED CHICKEN LEGS WITH PEA, LETTUCE, AND PANCETTA STEW

40
___
TOTAL

Preparation 10
Cooking 30
Serves 4

This is the easiest dish to cook with minimal shopping. It can be rustled up with things in the freezer such as chicken and petits pois. It's a good idea to keep the freezer stocked with bare essentials and take them out to thaw in the morning. All you then need to do is pick up some Boston lettuce and heavy cream on the way home.

4 chicken legs
2 tablespoons olive oil
1 teaspoon dried oregano
salt and freshly ground black pepper

For the pea, lettuce, and pancetta stew
4 tablespoons butter
1⅔ cups smoked lardons or pancetta cubes
2 shallots, peeled and finely sliced
2 garlic cloves, peeled and sliced

1 tablespoon all-purpose flour
4 heads of Boston lettuce, cut into quarters
½ cup white wine
1¼ cups chicken stock
3 cups frozen petits pois
a pinch of white sugar
⅓ cup plus 1 tablespoon heavy cream
juice of 1 lemon
loaf of crusty bread, to serve

1 Preheat the oven to 375°F. Start by preparing the chicken legs for roasting. To make sure you get a good crispy skin, rub the legs with the olive oil and season with the oregano and salt and pepper. Put into a roasting pan and roast for about 30 minutes, without turning them over, until the meat is cooked through.

2 When the chicken has been in the oven for 15 minutes, start to cook the pea, lettuce, and pancetta stew. Put the butter in a deep skillet or casserole dish and add the lardons or pancetta. Pan-fry until slightly golden, 5 to 6 minutes, before adding the shallots and garlic. Then add the flour and stir well. Season with salt and pepper.

3 Lay the lettuce in the pan, cut-side down, add the wine and stock, and bring to a boil. Then reduce the heat and let simmer until the liquid has reduced by half.

4 Add the peas with the sugar and cream. Bring the mixture up to a boil, stirring gently from time to time to stop anything on the bottom of the pan burning. If your mixture looks a bit dry, add a few tablespoons of water or chicken stock. Add the lemon juice and check for seasoning.

If you have cream cheese in the fridge, it makes a lovely sauce instead of using the heavy cream.

5 Remove the chicken from the oven and serve alongside the stew, with crusty bread to mop up the juices.

BAKED SALMON WITH PANCETTA, POTATOES, TOMATOES, AND ASPARAGUS

40
TOTAL

Preparation 10
Cooking 30
Serves 4

This isn't so much a recipe as a mixture of ingredients thrown together that taste great when combined and cook in about the same time. Salmon is a fish that can have a bit of a bad name as people tend to overcook it and serve it with the same old accompaniments. I promise that this combination of flavors and ingredients work in perfect harmony.

4 tablespoons olive oil, plus extra for oiling
8 potatoes
salt and freshly ground black pepper
2 teaspoons dried oregano
4 salmon fillets, weighing about
   5½ to 6 ounces each

20 spears of asparagus, trimmed
20 cherry plum tomatoes on the vine,
   halved
8 slices of pancetta or prosciutto
juice of 1 lemon

1 Preheat the oven to 375°F. Line a large baking sheet with parchment paper and rub with a little oil. Slice the potatoes (with their skins left on) to the thickness of about ⅛ inch. Lay the potatoes over the baking sheet, trying not to overlap them too much. Sprinkle generously with salt and pepper and the oregano and drizzle with 2 tablespoons of olive oil. Put in the hot oven for 15 minutes.

2 Remove the baking sheet from the oven and increase the temperature to 425°F. Lay the salmon fillets on top of the potatoes and scatter around the asparagus spears and tomatoes. Drape the pancetta or Parma ham over the top. Drizzle over the rest of the olive oil and put the pan back in the oven for an additional 10 to 15 minutes until everything is cooked through.

3 Squeeze over the lemon juice and serve immediately.

Great with chicken thighs or any meaty fish—I often use monkfish.

HONEY-ROASTED PORK TENDERLOIN WITH PEARS AND PARSNIPS

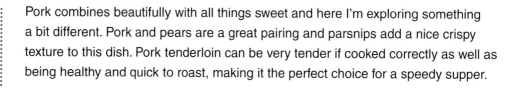

50
TOTAL

Preparation 15
Cooking 35
Serves 4 to 6

You can cook the pork in a skillet to caramelize the outside before transferring to the oven to finish cooking for 15 to 20 minutes.

Pork combines beautifully with all things sweet and here I'm exploring something a bit different. Pork and pears are a great pairing and parsnips add a nice crispy texture to this dish. Pork tenderloin can be very tender if cooked correctly as well as being healthy and quick to roast, making it the perfect choice for a speedy supper.

2 pork tenderloins, weighing about
   10½ to 14 ounces each
2 tablespoons whole-grain mustard
2 tablespoons honey
juice of 2 lemons
2 garlic cloves, peeled and chopped or
   2 teaspoons ready-chopped garlic

2 sprigs of thyme, leaves only
4 tablespoons olive oil
2 Comice pears, cored and cut into
   pieces lengthwise
4 parsnips, peeled and cut into pieces
   lengthwise
salt and freshly ground black pepper

1 Preheat the oven to 375°F. Lay the pork tenderloins in a wide container. Mix together the mustard, honey, lemon juice, garlic, thyme, and olive oil in a small bowl. Combine well and pour half the mixture over the pork. Cover and set aside.

2 Mix the pears and parsnips in a roasting pan and pour over the remaining honey and mustard mixture. Try to make sure the parsnips are closer to the edges of the pan, as these will take slightly longer to cook. Lay the pork on top and pour over the marinade. Season well with salt and pepper and roast in the oven for 35 minutes until the meat is cooked through and the parsnips are tender and slightly crispy.

3 Let the pork rest for 5 minutes before carving into slices. Serve with the roasted vegetables and the sauce from the roasting pan.

TANDOORI-MARINATED MACKEREL WITH RED ONION AND CILANTRO SALAD

25
TOTAL

Preparation 15
Cooking 10
Serves 2

I know there are lots of spices in this recipe, which can be expensive to buy, but once you have them you will use them again and again. Because I'm using this marinade on fish, you don't really have to marinate it at all, which helps speed up the prep time.

For the tandoori marinade
2 teaspoons ground cumin
2 teaspoons ground coriander
2 teaspoons turmeric
½ teaspoon ground cinnamon
2 teaspoons hot paprika
3 garlic cloves, peeled and crushed
2 red peppers
⅔ cup thick, set plain yogurt
juice of 2 lemons
salt and freshly ground black pepper

For the red onion and cilantro salad
3 red onions, peeled and finely
  sliced into rings

juice of 2 limes
1 teaspoon white sugar
½ teaspoon salt
a large bunch of cilantro, chopped
a handful of mint leaves, chopped
olive oil, for drizzling

For the mackerel
2 to 3 whole mackerel, gutted
juice of ½ lime

To serve
⅔ cup thick, set plain yogurt
1 lime, cut into wedges

1 Heat the broiler to medium. Make the marinade by combining all the ingredients with a large pinch of salt and pepper. Blend in a food processor until smooth. Set aside.

2 To make the salad, combine all the ingredients, except the cilantro, mint, and oil, and set aside for the flavors to infuse.

3 Take the mackerel and make three deep slashes on the diagonal on both sides of each fish. This will allow the marinade to penetrate the flesh of the fish and also speed up cooking time. Generously cover the fish with the marinade on both sides and lay them on a nonstick broiler pan so they are easy to turn over halfway through cooking.

4 Broil the fish for about 5 minutes before turning them over and cooking for an additional 5 minutes—the fish is ready when the skin starts to bubble and blister slightly. Insert a small knife into the thickest part of one of the incisions and see if the flesh easily comes away. Remove the mackerel from the broiler and squeeze over the lime juice.

5 Mix the cilantro and mint with the onion salad and drizzle with some olive oil. Serve with the fish accompanied by the yogurt and wedges of lime.

This marinade works well on most meats and is also fantastic on the barbecue —it can be made up to 3 to 4 days in advance and stored in the fridge ready to use.

GRILLED HAM STEAK, FRIED EGG, AND SPICY BEANS

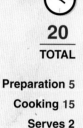

20

TOTAL

Preparation 5

Cooking 15

Serves 2

Breakfast at dinner time?! What else can I say—HEAVEN, and all in 20 minutes. This is my ultimate indulgent naughty feast and it's perfect for a lazy night's supper.

2 teaspoons prepared English mustard
1 teaspoon honey
3 tablespoons vegetable oil
salt and freshly ground black pepper
2 chunky ham steaks, weighing about 6 to 7 ounces each
2 large eggs

For the beans
1 x 14-ounce can black beans
1 cup strained tomatoes
1 teaspoon Worcestershire sauce
½ teaspoon Tabasco sauce
a small bunch of flatleaf parsley, coarsely chopped

1 Heat a grill pan or large skillet on high heat. Make the marinade by mixing the mustard, honey, and 1 tablespoon of oil together. Season with a pinch of salt and pepper and spread over the ham steaks while your grill pan or skillet heats up.

2 Once smoking hot, lay the steaks onto the grill pan or skillet and cook for 4 to 5 minutes on each side. If it looks like the marinade is charring slightly, move the steaks around in the pan and turn down the heat a little. Brush with any of the remaining marinade. Once the steaks have had their 8 to 10 minutes' cooking, turn off the heat and let them rest while you finish the rest of the meal.

3 This stage can be done while the ham steaks are cooking. Drain and rinse the beans, then add them to a saucepan with the strained tomatoes and Worcestershire and Tabasco sauces. Simmer for around 10 minutes, stirring from time to time to stop everything from sticking. Season to taste with salt and pepper. Once thickened and hot, sprinkle in the chopped parsley.

This makes a great breakfast—with a grilled tortilla and sprinkle of grated cheese, you don't even need the ham!

4 Finally, heat a skillet with 2 tablespoons vegetable oil and crack in the eggs. Season the yolks with salt and cook for about 3 minutes until still runny. Serve the fried eggs on top of the ham steaks and the beans on the side.

ROASTED POUSSIN WITH POMEGRANATE AND ALMOND COUSCOUS

45
<hr>
TOTAL

Preparation 10
plus 5 minutes
resting time
Cooking 35
Serves 4

Poussins are a great dinner time savior if you don't have time to roast a whole chicken. They cook in half the time and everyone gets their own bird, which means no fights about who gets the breast and who gets the leg! Just like a chicken, you can eat just about anything with them, and I've decided to do a bit of a Moroccan twist with this recipe. You will have a tasty dinner on the table within an hour of walking in the door.

2 lemons, cut in half
4 whole poussins
4 sprigs of thyme
scant ½ cup butter
salt and freshly ground black pepper

For the couscous
1⅔ cups vegetable stock

scant 1¼ cups couscous
½ teaspoon dried red pepper flakes
zest and juice of 2 lemons
½ bunch of cilantro, chopped
½ bunch of mint, leaves only, chopped
¾ cup toasted slivered almonds
heaping ¾ cup pomegranate seeds
3 tablespoons olive oil

1 Preheat the oven to 375°F. Start by cooking the poussins. Place a lemon half in the cavity of each bird along with a sprig of thyme in each. Soften the butter between your fingers and rub liberally all over the skin of each poussin. Season with salt and pepper, put into one or two roasting pans, and roast in the hot oven for about 35 minutes.

2 While they are roasting, prepare the couscous. Heat the stock in a saucepan. Put the couscous in a large bowl and add the red pepper flakes and some salt and pepper. Pour the stock over the couscous and cover with plastic wrap. Let stand for 10 to 15 minutes for the couscous to steam and swell.

3 Add the lemon zest and juice, chopped herbs, slivered almonds, and pomegranate seeds to the couscous. Then drizzle with the olive oil, use a fork to fluff up the couscous, and taste for seasoning. Set aside.

4 Once the poussins are cooked, remove from the oven and let rest for 5 minutes. Pour any drippings from the pan into the couscous before serving alongside the roasted birds.

Pomegranate seeds are available prepicked from supermarkets in the prepared fruit section and are a great time-saver to have in your fridge.

LAMB CHOPS WITH SMASHED WHITE BEAN CHAMP

20

TOTAL

Preparation 10

Cooking 10

Serves 4

This is a dinner that should become part of your weekly menu—it's inexpensive, uses pantry basics, involves hardly any preparation time, and tastes great. You can usually get lamb chops for a reasonable price and a can of lima beans is a very important pantry ingredient and therefore should always be available. My style of cooking tends to draw on a few main ingredients—in this case the lamb and the beans—and then I like to jazz things up a bit by adding fresh herbs or a few spices to make a normal evening meal come to life. This dish is no exception.

12 lamb chops
5 tablespoons extra virgin olive oil
2 tablespoons balsamic vinegar
3 garlic cloves, finely sliced
salt and freshly ground black pepper
⅓ cup butter
3 garlic cloves, peeled and grated

2 sprigs of rosemary, leaves only,
  finely chopped
juice of 1 lemon
2 x 14-ounce cans lima beans, drained
6 scallions, trimmed and finely sliced

1 Preheat the broiler to the highest setting. Place the lamb chops in a bowl with 2 tablespoons of the olive oil, all the vinegar, the sliced garlic, and a big pinch of salt and pepper. Rub in the marinade well before placing the lamb under the broiler and cooking for 5 minutes on each side.

2 While the lamb is cooking, melt the butter in a saucepan and add the garlic and rosemary. When the butter starts to bubble and go slightly nut brown in color, squeeze in the lemon juice and add the beans and scallions. Stir well until heated through.

3 Turn off the heat and mash the beans with a potato masher. You don't need a fine paste—lumps are good. Pour in most of the remaining olive oil or enough to get the consistency as you like it. It will be quite firm.

4 Once the lamb chops are cooked, let them rest and pour any drippings into the bean mash. Taste the mash for seasoning and serve with the lamb.

Great to serve when you have guests over. Try starting with the Corn and Scallion Fritters (see page 137) to whet a few appetites.

SHRIMP AND EGG FRIED RICE

20

TOTAL

Preparation 10
Cooking 10
Serves 4 to 6

I absolutely love egg fried rice but always avoided making it at home, as you have to cook the rice and then wait for it to cool. Then I discovered ready-cooked rice, which is perfect for this dish. The chef in me told me I should always avoid using preprepared foods, but here is one that is definitely allowed. You can add whatever you like to this dish; I love big, fat juicy shrimp in mine. If you want to bulk it out a bit, you can add other vegetables such as broccoli, snow peas, or green beans and cooked meats like chicken and pork... the list is endless.

2 x 8½-ounce pouches ready-cooked
  basmati rice
3 eggs
2 tablespoons vegetable or peanut oil
2 red chiles, coarsely sliced and seeds left
  in if you are a fan of spicy food
2 garlic cloves, peeled and coarsely
  chopped
6 scallions, trimmed and cut into
  ¾-inch pieces with the white and green
  parts separated

14 ounces medium raw shrimp, peeled
  and deveined
4 tablespoons dark soy sauce
1 teaspoon sesame oil
2 tablespoons sweet chili sauce
2 large handfuls of frozen or fresh peas
  (thawed if using frozen peas)
1 lime, cut into wedges
a large bunch of cilantro

1 To prepare the rice, follow the directions on the rice pouch (usually put it in the microwave for 2½ minutes).

2 Beat the eggs in a bowl. Heat a large wok or skillet on the stove, add the vegetable or peanut oil, and when the oil is very hot, add the chiles, garlic, and white part of the scallions and stir-fry for 2 minutes. Remove them from the pan, then add the beaten eggs and move them around quickly in the pan until cooked and well scrambled—I like to leave some big bits of egg, as this is the best part. Remove the scrambled eggs.

3 Add the cooked ingredients back into the pan along with the shrimp, heated rice, soy sauce, sesame oil, sweet chili sauce, green tips of the scallions, and the peas. Stir well and then add the egg back in and heat through for 3 to 4 minutes. Mix together well and serve with a wedge of lime and torn cilantro.

Raw shrimp give
the best flavor,
but if you are
in hurry, then
cooked shrimp
are fine for a
midweek dinner.

GRILLED SWORDFISH STEAK WITH CHERMOULA POTATO SALAD

35
TOTAL

Preparation 10
Cooking 25
Serves 4

Swordfish is a meaty fish that stands up well to strong flavors, making this perfumed chermoula the perfect match. This is a lovely light and healthy dish with tons of flavor. If you make an extra-large potato salad, it will be great for lunch the next day, therefore getting two meals out of the way in one cooking session. If you can't get swordfish, tuna or sea bass also work very well. Try mixing the chermoula with canned beans or using it as a marinade. It's great!

2¼ pounds new potatoes
4 swordfish steaks, ¾-inch thick and
  weighing about 4½ to 5½ ounces each
2 tablespoons olive oil
sea salt and freshly ground black pepper
juice of 1 lemon

For the chermoula
2 large bunches of cilantro, finely
  chopped

2 red peppers, finely chopped
4 garlic cloves, peeled and finely grated
2 teaspoons ground cumin
zest and juice of 2 lemons
6 tablespoons olive oil
1 teaspoon red wine vinegar
3½ ounces arugula

1 Cook the potatoes in boiling salted water until very tender.

2 To make the chermoula, mix the cilantro with the chiles and garlic in a large bowl. Add the cumin, lemon zest and juice, olive oil, vinegar, and salt and pepper. This can all be done in a blender if you prefer.

3 Once the potatoes are cooked, drain them and return them to the pan they were cooked in. Smash the potatoes with the back of a fork while still hot and pour over two-thirds of the chermoula.

4 Heat a grill pan until it smokes. Rub the swordfish steaks with a little olive oil and season with sea salt and pepper. Lay onto the hot grill pan and cook for 5 minutes on each side. Squeeze over the juice of the remaining lemon and turn off the heat.

5 Mix the arugula through the potato and chermoula mixture and divide among serving plates. Lay a swordfish steak on top of each and serve while still warm with the remaining chermoula on the side.

Make a little extra chermoula and it will keep for a week in the fridge. Put it into a clean canning jar and pour a couple of tablespoons of olive oil on top to stop the air getting to it.

BAKED GNOCCHI WITH HOT-SMOKED SALMON AND SPINACH

20
TOTAL

Preparation 5
Cooking 15
Serves 4 to 6

Try cooking the
Baked Apricot
Brioche (see page
144) for dessert.
Take the gnocchi
out of the oven and
put the brioche
straight in.

Gnocchi is that wonderful dish I order in a restaurant and wish I cooked more at home. The truth is that once you've gone through the process of making gnocchi, so much of the day is lost. Now that's fine if it's raining outside and you have a whole day to spend in the kitchen, but you should know that store-bought gnocchi is just as good as store-bought pasta (they are both available in the same section of the supermarket), and we all buy that. This dish has a sharp tang to it and makes a good change from having pasta.

1 x 14-ounce bag young spinach leaves
scant 1 cup mascarpone cheese
zest and juice of 2 lemons
2¾ ounces fresh dill weed, chopped

salt and freshly ground black pepper
10½ ounces hot-smoked salmon
18 ounces fresh gnocchi
¾ cup grated Parmesan cheese

1 Preheat the broiler to high and bring a large pot of water with a big pinch of salt added to a boil.

2 Make 2 to 3 holes in the bag of spinach and put it in the microwave at for 2 minutes until wilted. If you don't have a microwave, then steam the spinach until it is slightly wilted.

3 Put the mascarpone cheese into a saucepan and add the lemon zest and juice and dill weed, and season with salt and pepper. Stir over low heat until the mascarpone has melted, then add the wilted spinach and flake in the salmon. Try to keep the salmon pieces quite big.

4 Put the gnocchi into the pot of boiling water and cook for 3 minutes. Drain and return to the pot, then stir in the salmon and spinach sauce. Pour the whole lot into a baking dish and cover with the grated Parmesan. Broil for 3 to 5 minutes until the top bubbles and is golden brown.

SPICY BEEF SAUSAGE AND RICOTTA NAAN PIZZAS

25
TOTAL

Preparation 10
Cooking 15
Serves 4

**Try with My
Chop Salad on
the side (see
page 129).**

We all love pizza—it's loaded with everything we like and, best of all, it's one of the few dinners we are allowed to eat with our fingers. But pizza dough is really something that needs time, and let's face it, time is something that a lot of us don't often have. So this is my own quick version and I love it! If you can't find the spicy beef sausage, you can spice it up with sliced pepperoni or by adding some chopped chiles.

2 tablespoons tomato paste
4 naan (plain or flavored)
¾ cup ricotta cheese
4 uncooked spicy beef sausages
2 red onions, peeled and finely
   sliced into rings

4 pinches of dried red pepper flakes
4 pinches of ground cumin
salt and freshly ground black pepper
2 tablespoons olive oil, plus extra
   for drizzling
3½ ounces arugula

1 Preheat the oven to 425°F. Mix the tomato paste with 2 tablespoons of water to loosen it and spread a small amount over each naan. Leave a border around the edge as you would with a pizza.

2 Crumble the ricotta cheese onto each naan. Remove the sausage from the casings and evenly distribute the meat among all four naan. Scatter over the onion slices and add a pinch of red pepper flakes and ground cumin to each one. Season with salt and lots of pepper. Drizzle with the olive oil and place in the hot oven for 15 minutes.

3 Remove the naans from the oven, scatter with the arugula, and drizzle with a little more olive oil. Serve immediately.

Watching Your Pennies

When times are tough and money is a bit tight, going out to eat is an expense that few people can afford. I want to give a few tips on how to make a great dinner without having to spend a fortune and, of course, in quick time. This chapter should appeal to all your family and friends. If you're really smart about what you cook, where you buy your food, and use seasonal ingredients when possible, you can make some fantastic tasty food while still on a budget. If you're cooking for friends, make sure they bring the wine!

CHICKEN AND LIMA BEAN CASSOULET

60
___
TOTAL

Preparation 5
Cooking 55
Serves 4

Chicken thighs are extremely reasonable to buy and have a much better flavor than the breast. They don't dry out while cooking and lend themselves very well to slow-cooked dishes. The great thing about this dish is that once the minimal chopping and browning is done there is very little left for you to do, allowing you the luxury of time to relax while your dinner cooks.

2 tablespoons vegetable oil
4 chicken thighs
4 chicken drumsticks
salt and freshly ground black pepper
7 ounces smoked lardons or smoked
  bacon slices, chopped
1 large red onion, peeled and finely diced
3 garlic cloves, peeled and sliced
1 bay leaf
1 teaspoon dried oregano

1 tablespoon tomato paste
2 x 14-ounce cans lima beans, drained
  and rinsed
½ cup white wine
2 x 14-ounce cans plum tomatoes
1 teaspoon white sugar
heaping 1 cup dry bread crumbs
¾ cup grated Parmesan cheese

1 Preheat the oven to 400°F. Heat a large, deep skillet or an ovenproof casserole dish on high heat with the vegetable oil. Season the chicken with salt and pepper and gently pan-fry until all sides are golden brown, about 5 minutes in total.

2 Remove the chicken from the pan, wipe out any slightly burned bits with paper towels, and add the lardons or bacon. Increase the heat and let the bacon crisp a little. Add the onion with the garlic and cook until softened. Then add the bay leaf and oregano followed by the tomato paste and mix well. Finally, add the lima beans and give it one more stir.

3 Return the chicken to the pan, mix around well, and pour in the white wine and the plum tomatoes. The stew now needs to simmer slowly for 25 minutes. Season with the sugar and salt and pepper.

4 Once the mixture starts to thicken, reduce the heat and sprinkle with the bread crumbs and Parmesan cheese. Put in the hot oven, uncovered, for 15 to 20 minutes until the bread crumbs are nice and crispy. Serve immediately.

**A great
alternative is to
substitute the
chicken with
monkfish or
some peeled
jumbo shrimp.**

PAN–ROASTED BEETS, SOFT GOAT CHEESE, MINT, AND FAVA BEAN SALAD

20
TOTAL

Preparation 10

Cooking 10

Serves 2
as a light dinner
or 4 as a side dish

This is a colorful and lively dish that will please most people. It is lovely as a healthy dinner on its own, and is so quick and easy that it can also be made as a side dish to accompany your main meal. Buy good-quality young goat cheese to ensure a nice fresh flavor, and if you can't get hold of fava beans, soybeans are also very good. Beets are often overlooked as a vegetable and I think that this simple dish really does them justice.

1 tablespoon olive oil
8 small ready-cooked beets, cut into
   quarters
2 tablespoons balsamic vinegar
3 sprigs of fresh thyme, leaves only
a pinch of white sugar
⅔ cup fava beans or soybeans (fresh if in
   season or frozen)
a bunch of mint, leaves only, finely
   shredded

½ cup toasted hazelnuts, lightly crushed
7 ounces soft goat cheese
a small handful of basil leaves

For the dressing
1 tablespoon Dijon mustard
zest and juice of 1 lemon
1 tablespoon honey
2 tablespoons olive oil
salt and freshly ground black pepper

1 Preheat a skillet with the olive oil. Put the beets into the pan and season with salt. Cook on high heat for 6 minutes until the beets are charred on the edges, then add the balsamic vinegar, thyme leaves, and sugar. Turn down the heat and let the beets color some more, an additional 3 to 5 minutes.

2 Remove the beets from the pan, reduce the heat to the lowest setting, and add the ingredients for the dressing to the pan drippings. Mix well and season with salt and pepper. Remove from the heat.

For a quicker alternative to chopping the hazelnuts, wrap them in plastic wrap and crush using a rolling pin or the base of a saucepan.

3 If the fava or soybeans are frozen, put them in a heatproof bowl, pour a kettle of boiling water over them to thaw, then drain. Put the beans back into the bowl and lightly crush with the back of a fork, keeping some whole. Then add the shredded mint leaves and hazelnuts and pour over half the dressing from the skillet.

4 Scatter the warm caramelized beets over a big platter, crumble over the soft goat cheese, and scatter over the crushed bean and mint mixture. Pour over the remaining warm dressing and sprinkle with the basil leaves. Serve immediately.

MINUTE STEAK SANDWICH WITH FRIED ONIONS AND SWEET MUSTARD

20
TOTAL

Preparation 5
Cooking 15
Serves 1
as a light dinner or
2 as a side dish

Accompany with the Chunky Potato Wedges (see page 123) and finish with An Easy Mess (see page 151).

A very thin pan-frying steak is the most economical quick-cook steak you'll find and it is most definitely the best for a big hearty sandwich. This is such a naughty dinner, but it's perfect for a night in on your own.

2 tablespoons vegetable oil
2 large onions, peeled and sliced
2 very thin minute steaks, weighing
   4 ounces each
salt and freshly ground black pepper

1 ciabatta or baguette, or your preferred
   bread, toasted
2 tablespoons butter, softened
2 tablespoons yellow mustard

1 Place a skillet on the stove and add half the oil along with the onions. Pan-fry on high heat until golden brown and a bit crispy around the edges, 10 minutes.

2 Move the cooked onions over to the edge of the pan and increase the heat. Add another tablespoon of oil. Season the steaks on both sides with salt and pepper and put them in the pan. Cook for 45 seconds on each side. Turn off the heat and take the steaks out of the pan to rest.

3 Cut your chosen bread in half and toast on both sides either on a grill pan or under the broiler. Spread with butter and loads of mustard. Pile on the onions and slice the steak before loading onto the sandwich. Put on the top half of toasted bread and dunk into more mustard while you eat.

CORNED BEEF HASH FRITTATA

Eggs are a great base for a variety of ingredients and you can add just about anything to a frittata—try chorizo, smoked paprika, and roasted bell peppers as well.

2 large potatoes, peeled and cut into
    ½-inch cubes
salt and freshly ground black pepper
1 tablespoon vegetable oil
2 large onions, peeled and sliced

2 x 7-ounce cans corned beef, cut into
    ½-inch cubes
2 tablespoons Worcestershire sauce
4 eggs
ketchup, to serve (optional)

45
TOTAL

Preparation 10
Cooking 35
Serves 2
as a light dinner
or 4 to 6 as a side dish

Red-skinned
potatoes are
good for this
dish, as they
hold together
well when
cooked.

1 Preheat the oven to 350°F. Put the potatoes in a saucepan, add boiling water from the kettle and a big pinch of salt, and cook until tender, about 8 minutes.

2 Meanwhile, heat the biggest ovenproof nonstick skillet you have and add the vegetable oil. Add the onions to the pan and cook until soft, 6 to 7 minutes (it's okay if they color a bit).

3 Drain the potatoes and add these to the onions. Cook for an additional 5 minutes before adding the corned beef. Heat through and stir in the Worcestershire sauce and lots of salt and pepper.

4 Beat the eggs in a bowl, increase the heat under the corned beef and potatoes, and pour in the egg mixture. Stir around in the pan until the egg starts to set, about 5 minutes. Transfer the pan to the oven and cook for about 15 minutes until the egg is almost completely set. Serve with a big dollop of ketchup, if you wish.

PENNE AND SAUSAGE RAGÙ

50
TOTAL

Preparation 10
Cooking 40
Serves 4

Here is a fantastic quick-time ragù recipe that makes a great change to the old staple spaghetti Bolognese. It is lovely to make and store a stash of in the freezer, ready to thaw in serious pasta emergencies. I cook this regularly, always with a slight difference, but the basics always stay the same—onions, garlic, canned tomatoes, and the good old humble sausage (I like to use a spicy herb variety).

1 tablespoon olive oil
1 large red onion, peeled and finely
  chopped
½ teaspoon dried red pepper flakes
3 garlic cloves, peeled and finely chopped
salt and freshly ground black pepper
1 bay leaf
4 good-quality sausages of your choosing

1 tablespoon tomato paste
½ cup red wine
1 x 14-ounce can diced tomatoes
1 teaspoon balsamic vinegar
½ teaspoon white sugar
2 tablespoons mascarpone cheese
4⅔ cups (18 ounces) dry penne
Parmesan cheese shavings, to serve

1 Place a large skillet or casserole dish on medium heat and pour in the olive oil. Add the onion, red pepper flakes, and garlic followed by a pinch of salt. Tear the bay leaf slightly and add to the onion mix, then let everything cook gently for 5 to 6 minutes.

2 Meanwhile, remove the sausage from the casings and break up the meat. Increase the heat under the onions and add the sausage meat. Stir around in the onions until the meat starts to color, then add the tomato paste and mix well. Try to break up the sausage meat as much as you can in the pan and stop it clumping into meaty lumps.

3 Pour in the wine, tomatoes, and vinegar and stir in the sugar and mascarpone. Season again and let the mixture boil and bubble for about 15 minutes. Stir occasionally to prevent the ragù sticking to the bottom of the pan. Reduce the heat and let the mixture simmer away gently while you cook the pasta.

4 Put a big pot of water on the stove to boil and add a pinch of salt. When the water starts to boil, add the pasta and cook as directed on the package until al dente. Drain the pasta, return it to the pot, and add the sausage ragù.

5 Divide among four plates and serve with Parmesan shavings over the top.

For a change,
try adding
mozzarella and
fresh basil to
the ragù just
before serving.

TURKEY SCALLOPINE WITH SAGE BUTTER

25
___
TOTAL

Preparation 10
Cooking 15
Serves 2

This recipe is particularly simple to prepare, requiring little peeling or chopping. Turkey scallopine are far less expensive to buy than chicken breasts (they are sometimes called turkey breast steaks) and taste just as good.

2 turkey scallopine
4 tablespoons all-purpose flour
1 large egg
8 tablespoons dry bread crumbs
salt and freshly ground black pepper

6 tablespoons vegetable oil
1/3 cup butter
8 to 10 sage leaves
juice of 1 lemon

1 The turkey scallopine need to be as thin as possible. So if they're looking a bit chunky, put them into a plastic bag, lay flat, and give them a good bashing with a rolling pin until they are about 1/16 inch thick all over.

2 Put the flour, egg, and bread crumbs into separate bowls. Season the flour well, then place the scallopine first into the seasoned flour, then coat well in the egg, and finally in the bread crumbs.

3 Heat a large skillet on high heat and pour in all the oil. When the oil is hot, lay in the breaded turkey scallopine and cook for 4 to 5 minutes on each side until golden brown.

4 Remove them from the pan with a slotted spoon or spatula and lay onto paper towels. Pour the oil from the pan into a glass jar or container and let cool before throwing it away. Place the skillet back on the stove on medium heat and add the butter. When the butter starts to foam, add the sage leaves and lemon juice and cook for an additional 20 to 30 seconds.

5 To serve, put the scallopine onto individual plates and pour over the foaming butter. Add spoonfuls of the Gorgonzola Polenta alongside, if you like.

Try serving with the Gorgonzola Polenta (see page 23).

ZUCCHINI, BASIL, AND CHILE LINGUINE WITH CRÈME FRAÎCHE

A healthy and tasty meal that can be prepared in minutes. You don't need to resort to takeout or premade dinners—this dish can be on the table within 20 minutes of walking through the door.

20
TOTAL

Preparation 5
Cooking 15
Serves 4

Try using cooked ham and a few fresh peas when in season.

18 ounces dry linguine
2 tablespoons olive oil, plus extra to drizzle
½ teaspoon dried red pepper flakes
2 garlic cloves, peeled and chopped
4 large zucchini, coarsely shredded
juice of 1 lemon

15 basil leaves
4 to 5 tablespoons crème fraîche or sour cream
salt and freshly ground black pepper
1 cup grated Parmesan cheese

1 Put a big pot of water on the stove to boil and add a pinch of salt. When the water starts to boil, add the pasta and cook as directed on the package until al dente.

2 Heat the olive oil in a small pan on very low heat with the red pepper flakes and garlic. Turn off the heat once they start to cook and bubble.

3 Drain the pasta and return it to the pan it was cooked in. Stir in the red pepper flakes, garlic, and warmed olive oil. Then add the zucchini, lemon juice, and basil and stir through the crème fraîche or sour cream. Season well with salt and pepper. Serve with a drizzle of olive oil and the grated Parmesan cheese.

A BIG BOWL OF CURRIED MUSSELS

25

TOTAL

Preparation 10
Cooking 15
Serves 4

Mussels are a fabulous inexpensive product. They are instant food and very good for you, too. And few foods give you your very own pair of tongs to use while eating as well, so there's no need for cutlery—just use an empty shell.

5½ pounds live mussels, scrubbed
1 tablespoon vegetable oil
2 shallots, peeled and sliced
¼ teaspoon chili powder
½ teaspoon ground cumin

1 tablespoon medium curry powder
¾ cup plus 1 tablespoon coconut milk
2 limes, 1 freshly squeezed for its juice
   and the other cut into wedges
½ bunch of cilantro

1 Place all the mussels into a sink of cold water. Sort through them, throwing away any that may be broken or open. To check if the mussel is alive, tap its shell on the surface: if the open mussel closes, it's alive and fine to eat; if it doesn't close, throw it away. While you are doing this, pull off any "beards" that may be clinging to the mussels.

2 Put a large pan with a tight-fitting lid on the stove and add the vegetable oil. Add the shallots and gently sauté until translucent. Sprinkle in all the spices and mix well in the pan. Cook for 5 minutes to let the flavor of the spices develop.

3 Add all the mussels and the coconut milk to the pan and turn the heat up to high. Put on the lid and cook the mussels for 5 to 6 minutes, shaking the pan regularly, until heated through and the mussels have all opened up (discard any that won't open).

These are great with Chunky Potato Wedges (see page 123).

4 Transfer the mussels to four large bowls together with the pot liquid. Squeeze over the juice of 1 lime and tear in the cilantro leaves. Serve with another wedge of lime on the side if you wish.

LAMB'S LIVER WITH BACON AND SWEET POTATO MASH

35
TOTAL

Preparation 15
Cooking 20
Serves 4

Liver is a fantastic ingredient—inexpensive and very quick to cook. I've suggested lamb's liver, but if you are feeling flush, try calf's liver instead. However, the best part about this dish is the cheat's way of cooking the sweet potato mash; no peeling or boiling water needed here. Just a little gentle scooping and you're done. Have a go... you'll never make normal mash again.

4 sweet potatoes
4 smoked bacon slices, finely chopped
2 tablespoons olive oil
2 shallots, peeled and finely chopped
scant ½ cup butter

salt and freshly ground black pepper
2 tablespoons sour cream
4 thick slices of lamb's liver, weighing
  about 3½ to 4½ ounces each
3 tablespoons balsamic vinegar

1 Take the sweet potatoes and make three or four small stab marks all over them. Put into the microwave and cook at 800W for 15 minutes.

2 While they are cooking, heat a skillet and add the bacon. Turn the heat to medium and let it crisp and caramelize. After 5 to 6 minutes, add 1 tablespoon of the olive oil and the shallots and cook with the bacon for about 5 minutes until the shallots are soft and translucent. This will make the shallots super sweet. Turn off the heat if they are ready before the sweet potatoes.

3 When you hear the ping of the microwave, check to see if the potatoes are very tender and squashy inside. If not, give them a few more minutes. Once cooked, remove the potatoes and cut them in half. Using a spoon, scoop out the filling into a bowl.

Cook large baking potatoes in the microwave and, when really soft, scoop out the insides, then add butter, sour cream, and some chopped scallions for quick, hassle-free champ.

4 Turn on the heat under the bacon and shallots again and add two-thirds of the butter. When it has melted, transfer the bacon and shallot mixture to the bowl with the sweet potato filling and mash using a fork or a potato masher. Season well with lots of pepper but go easy on the salt, as the bacon is already salty. Finally, add the sour cream, mix well, and set aside while you cook the liver.

5 Place the skillet back on the highest heat and pour in the remaining olive oil. Season the liver with salt and pepper and put it in the hot pan. Cook for 2 minutes on each side. During the final minute of cooking, add the remaining butter and the vinegar.

6 Serve the liver with the sweet potato mash, drizzled with the pan drippings.

TASTY LAMB STEW

50–60
TOTAL

Preparation 10
Cooking 40–50
Serves 6 to 8

A really tasty
alternative to
the lamb stock
is a couple of
cans of beef
consommé.

Effectively an Irish stew but I didn't want to offend anyone by changing the recipe slightly to be as simple as possible using the good old bare bones of this classic, tasty stew. It is a stew to warm you from the inside out. It's comfort food for me and sometimes only comfort will do.

2½ quarts lamb stock
1 pound lamb tenderloin fillets, cut into 1¼-inch chunks
14 ounces potatoes, peeled and coarsely cut into 1¼-inch chunks
2 bay leaves
3 carrots, peeled and cut into sticks
2 leeks, trimmed, white part coarsely chopped

2 large onions, peeled and coarsely chopped
2 celery stalks, trimmed and coarsely chopped
salt and freshly ground black pepper
a small handful parsley, chopped

1 Put the stock in a large saucepan on medium heat and add the lamb. Bring to the boil and skim off any impurities before adding the potatoes and bay leaves. Reduce the heat and let the stew simmer for 10 minutes.

2 Add all the remaining vegetables, season with salt and pepper, and let simmer for an additional 30 to 40 minutes until everything is cooked through. Before serving, sprinkle the parsley on top.

TUNA, RED ONION, AND BEAN SALAD WITH A SOFT-BOILED EGG

15
___
TOTAL

Preparation 10
Cooking 5
Serves 2

Why not make this a more substantial meal by serving with An Easy Tart (see page 133)? You can take any leftovers to work for lunch the next day.

A super-simple throw-together meal that costs just pennies, this is a perfect weeknight dinner. We should all have these ingredients in our pantry or lurking in the bottom of the fridge, so it requires little shopping, making it a brilliant standby recipe.

2 large eggs
10½ ounces green beans, trimmed
1 x 7-ounce can tuna in water, drained
1 x 8-ounce can borlotti beans, drained
1 red onion, peeled and finely sliced
1 bag mixed salad leaves

salt and freshly ground black pepper

For the dressing
1 tablespoon red wine vinegar
1 tablespoon Dijon mustard
2 tablespoons olive oil

1 Bring a small saucepan of water to a boil. Carefully put the eggs into the water, reduce the temperature, and simmer for exactly 4 minutes 30 seconds. Add the green beans for the last minute of cooking. Remove the pan from the stove, drain into a colander, and run cold water over to cool.

2 Mix the tuna and the borlotti beans in a serving bowl and then add the green beans and the red onion.

3 Make the dressing by combining all the ingredients in a small bowl and pour three-quarters over the tuna mixture.

4 Carefully peel the eggs—they will be very soft, so make sure you don't break them.

5 Mix the salad leaves through the tuna salad and dress with the rest of the dressing. To finish, cut open the eggs and place two halves on each plate, seasoning with a pinch of salt and pepper.

CARAMELIZED CHICKEN

25

TOTAL

Preparation 5

Cooking 20

Serves 2

This is the perfect midweek supper. It's tasty, inexpensive, and quick to prepare. Everyone will love it, and when you've made it once, you can be as experimental with it as you like. This is a recipe that will be in your repertoire for years to come.

For the marinade
1 teaspoon dried thyme
2 tablespoons dark brown sugar
3 tablespoons Worcestershire sauce
½ teaspoon dried red pepper flakes or chili paste
2 tablespoons balsamic vinegar
2 tablespoons dark soy sauce
2 tablespoons ketchup

3 tablespoons olive oil

For the chicken
4 chicken legs
4 large red onions, peeled and cut into wedges
10 cherry tomatoes on the vine
4 large baking potatoes, to serve

1 Preheat the oven to 400°F. Put all the marinade ingredients in a big plastic bag and add the chicken and the onion wedges. Shake around so that all the ingredients get well coated in the marinade.

This homely dish has to be followed by the Banana Pudding with Toffee Sauce (see page 155).

2 When you are ready to cook, put the chicken legs into a roasting dish with the marinade, onions, and tomatoes. Cook in the oven for 15 to 20 minutes until the chicken is cooked through. The tomatoes should burst and the onions will go crispy around the edges. Meanwhile, cook the potatoes in the microwave at 800W for 8 minutes—add to the oven with the chicken when they are done to crisp up the skins.

3 To serve, put the potatoes on plates and add the chicken, roast tomatoes, and onion together with the marinade.

BASIL, PINE NUT, AND PARMESAN RISOTTO

30
TOTAL

Preparation 10
Cooking 20
Serves 4

This is effectively a pesto risotto, which is one of my favorites. I always think a risotto should be packed with relatively simple yet strong-flavored ingredients to make it interesting and exciting but not overly complex. For this recipe, the pesto is made by just throwing all the ingredients in without processing them. Nice and easy!

1½ quarts vegetable or chicken stock
2 tablespoons olive oil
1 leek, trimmed and white part finely chopped
2 garlic cloves, peeled and finely chopped
salt
1¾ cups risotto rice
4 tablespoons butter

¾ cup plus 1 tablespoon white wine
⅔ cup toasted pine nuts
1 tablespoon mascarpone cheese
a large handful of basil leaves
1 cup grated Parmesan cheese, plus a little extra for shaving
zest of 2 lemons

1 Heat up the stock on the stove and leave to one side with a ladle in the pan ready to feed the risotto in a few minutes' time.

2 Place a large, deep-sided casserole dish or skillet on the stove and heat to low temperature. Add the olive oil to the pan along with the leek and garlic. Add a pinch of salt and cook until soft, 3 to 5 minutes. Pour in the rice, add the butter, and stir well to coat all the rice grains in the butter and oil.

3 Increase the heat under the pan and add the white wine. Stir the rice until all the wine has been absorbed. Then add a ladleful of stock. You must stir at all times. Keep adding the stock a little at a time until the rice is cooked but still has a slight bite to it.

4 When you are happy with the texture of your risotto, add the pine nuts, mascarpone, torn basil leaves, Parmesan cheese, and lemon zest. Stir in well and serve with a few extra shavings of the cheese.

If really pushed for time you can use store-bought pesto but try to buy it from the deli or refrigerated section to ensure a fresh flavor and vibrant color.

SMOKED MACKEREL, NEW POTATO, AND HORSERADISH SALAD

Smoked mackerel keeps for ages in the fridge, so it's not only inexpensive but also has a long shelf life—something of a bonus if you don't get to the supermarket as often as you might like. Horseradish is an essential in everyone's fridge and, well, we all need potatoes. Serve this dish with a green salad.

20

TOTAL

Preparation 5
Cooking 15
Serves 4

Crème fraîche and sour cream are both available in whole and light versions. The light is just as tasty and fine to use in this recipe if you wish.

15 to 20 new potatoes, halved if quite large
4 smoked mackerel fillets
2¾ ounces chives, snipped
2 tablespoons hot horseradish sauce

2 tablespoons crème fraîche or sour cream
juice of 1 lemon
2 teaspoons mustard seeds
salt and freshly ground black pepper

1 Place a pan of water on the stove and bring to a boil. Add a pinch of salt and the potatoes. Bring back up to the boil, then reduce the heat and let simmer until tender, 10 to 12 minutes. Drain and return to the pan.

2 While the potatoes are still warm, flake in the mackerel fillets along with the chives, horseradish, and crème fraîche or sour cream. Add the lemon juice, mustard seeds, and salt and pepper.

CHUNKY HAM, WHITE BEAN, AND LEEK CASSEROLE

25

TOTAL

Preparation 10

Cooking 15

Serves 4

This recipe contains my favorite discovery yet—go to the deli counter at your grocery store and ask for ham ends. Sometimes they have them on display and sometimes not, but they are the odd nobbly bits that can't be used to make the perfect slice of ham when they carve the meat off the bone, so they never get used. They are brilliant and such an affordable way to bulk out an evening meal. Throw them into soups, pies, or this casserole.

4 tablespoons butter
3 whole leeks, trimmed and white parts cut into thin slices
2 x 14-ounce cans cannellini beans (although any other white beans will do), drained
14 ounces fully cooked ham ends (see above) or slices, cut into chunks

2 cups vegetable stock
2 tablespoons cream cheese
2 tablespoons whole-grain mustard
salt and freshly ground black pepper
1 lemon
crusty bread, to serve (optional)

1 Put a casserole dish or saucepan onto the stove on medium heat. Add the butter and then the leeks and cook them until they have wilted and softened, about 10 minutes. Keep stirring so they don't burn.

2 Add the beans and the ham along with the vegetable stock, cream cheese, and the mustard. Season with lots of black pepper but take it easy on the salt, as the ham will be quite salty—you may find you don't need any at all. Bring the sauce to a boil before adding a squeeze of lemon juice. (If you are using ham steaks, let the stew simmer for 30 minutes before adding the lemon juice for the meat to become tender.)

3 Serve in bowls alongside slices of crusty bread, if you wish.

This dish is just as good, if not better, the next day for a really warming lunch.

SMOKED HADDOCK PILAF

50
TOTAL

Preparation 15
Cooking 35
Serves 4

Technically, this dish is called kedgeree and is eaten at breakfast time, but as rice and spices first thing in the morning don't necessarily appeal to everyone, I've changed the name and made a few simple changes to make this a classic evening dish. This is easy cooking, with just a little chopping, then adding a few different spices, and throwing everything in the oven. Kedgeree is traditionally made with haddock but substitute with smoked trout if that's easier to find.

3¼ cups chicken stock
2 large or 3 small undyed smoked
   haddock (or trout) fillets
2 tablespoons vegetable oil
4 tablespoons butter
3 large onions, peeled and sliced
salt and freshly ground black pepper

1 teaspoon turmeric
2 teaspoons medium curry powder
2¼ cups basmati rice
4 teaspoons golden raisins
a small bunch of cilantro, chopped or torn
4 soft-boiled eggs, peeled and halved
   (optional)

1 Preheat the oven to 350°F. Pour the stock into a large saucepan and add the smoked haddock. Turn on the heat and bring the stock to a boil. As soon as it starts to boil, remove the pan from the heat and let cool.

2 Place a shallow casserole dish on medium heat and add the oil and butter. Cook the onions until they have softened, 4 to 5 minutes. Season well with 1 teaspoon of salt and plenty of black pepper.

3 Add the turmeric and the curry powder followed by the rice and the golden raisins. Stir well to coat the rice with the spices.

4 Remove the haddock from the pan and place it on a plate to one side. Pour the pot liquid into the casserole.

5 Put on a lid, if you have one, or improvise with aluminum foil and transfer to the oven. Cook for 20 to 25 minutes until all the liquid has been absorbed and the rice is tender. Check after 10 minutes, as you may need to add a little more stock if the rice is looking dry and still not cooked. When the rice is 5 minutes from being cooked—tender but still with a little bite to it—then flake in the smoked fish, being careful to avoid bones and skin. Stir into the rice and cook for an additional 5 minutes.

6 Sprinkle with the chopped or torn cilantro before you serve. Place the soft-boiled eggs on top, if using.

This can be cooked, covered, on low heat on the stovetop if you don't have enough time to wait for the oven to preheat.

MINESTRONE STEW

35
TOTAL

Preparation 15
Cooking 20
Serves 4

This is a brilliant dinner that the whole family can enjoy. Even though it's classically called a soup, this recipe is definitely substantial enough to be eaten as your main meal because it's more of a thick stew. The pasta and high vegetable content makes it a wholesome dinner.

2 tablespoons olive oil
9 ounces smoked lardons or smoked bacon slices, chopped
2 carrots, peeled and chopped into ½-inch dice
2 celery stalks, trimmed and chopped into ½-inch dice
2 zucchini, chopped into ½-inch dice
1 large onion, peeled and chopped into ½-inch dice
1 garlic clove, peeled and chopped or 1 teaspoon ready-chopped garlic
4 large ripe tomatoes, quartered
1 bay leaf

a pinch of dried red pepper flakes
2 sprigs of thyme, leaves only
2 tablespoons tomato paste
1½ quarts chicken or vegetable stock (made from a bouillon cube or ready-made store-bought stock)
salt and freshly ground black pepper
1¾ cups (7 ounces) conchigliette (tiny baby shell pasta)
4 outer leaves of savoy cabbage, shredded

To serve
crusty bread (optional)
Parmesan cheese shavings (optional)

1 Pour the olive oil into a large saucepan over medium heat. Add the lardons or chopped bacon and cook until slightly golden brown, 3 to 4 minutes. Then add the vegetables, garlic, and tomatoes, but not the cabbage. Also add the bay leaf, red pepper flakes, thyme, and tomato paste. Stir everything around well in the pan until all the vegetables are coated in the tomato paste.

2 Add the stock, increase the heat, and bring the soup to a boil. Then add salt and pepper followed by the pasta. Let the soup boil until the pasta is tender, about 10 minutes. You may need to add a little more stock or water just to cover the pasta completely. Once the pasta is cooked, add the cabbage and cook until it has wilted, 2 to 3 minutes.

3 Serve the soup either with crusty bread or just as it is—I personally like to add a little shaved Parmesan cheese and another twist of black pepper.

Make in big batches and freeze leftovers for a great instant dinner.

CREAMY MACARONI AND CHEESE

30
TOTAL

Preparation 5
Cooking 25
Serves 4

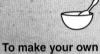

To make your own bread crumbs, cut an old loaf of bread into ¾–1¼-inch chunks. Place on a baking sheet, drizzle with olive oil, and bake in an oven at 375°F for 5 to 6 minutes. Remove from the oven and process in a food processor into crumbs.

Macaroni and cheese has to be one of the top ten comfort foods. The problem with the traditional macaroni and cheese recipe is that it involves making a cheese sauce, which is fine if you have the time, but I know many people who often don't. This recipe is a bit of a cheat, but that's what we like. It's also really good made with ham, cooked chicken, or even mushrooms.

18 ounces fresh or dry macaroni or penne
3½ ounces Boursin
3 tablespoons cream cheese
9 ounces mozzarella cheese

a large handful of basil leaves
4 handfuls of bread crumbs
½ cup grated Parmesan cheese

1 Preheat the broiler to medium. Bring a large pot of water to a boil, add a pinch of salt, and then add the pasta. Cook for 3 to 4 minutes if fresh, or according to the package directions if dry until al dente.

2 Put the Boursin and cream cheese in a small saucepan. Heat it and mix well until the Boursin has melted into a sauce. Drain the pasta, leaving a little of the water in the bottom of the pan. Return the pasta to the pan and add the melted Boursin and cream cheese. Tear in the mozzarella, add the basil leaves, and pour into a baking dish. Sprinkle with the bread crumbs and the Parmesan cheese and broil until golden brown. Serve immediately.

Posh Nosh

Just because you may have had a busy day doesn't mean you shouldn't be able to cook a few close friends or someone special a lovely dinner. In this chapter, I'm going to show you how you can prepare an elegant dinner that takes no time at all to create. If you are entertaining, you want to be in the kitchen for as little time as possible so that you have more time to spend with your guests. My key advice when preparing a slightly "posher" dinner is try to get a step ahead of the game. This could mean for instance laying the table the night before, so when you come home and start cooking, the detail that can often throw you is already done. Also, make sure you know the recipe—just have a quick read through before you start cooking. This way you will be a bit more familiar with it and cooking will be a far more enjoyable experience.

ROASTED HALIBUT WITH LENTIL AND SEMI-DRIED TOMATO RAGÙ

35–40
TOTAL

Preparation 20
Cooking 15–20
Serves 2

This fish dish is fragrant, fresh, and extremely simple to prepare. You can, of course, use dried lentils to make this recipe and it will only add about 15 minutes to the cooking time, but when you can buy them already cooked and you've had a long day, why bother? If you've got 10 minutes free the day before, there is plenty in this recipe that can be done in advance to make things easier when you come home the following night. Halibut is a meaty, silky smooth fish that is very forgiving to cook and very satisfying to eat. It is great for a special occasion or just when you feel like spoiling yourself.

For the ragù
2 cups precooked Puy lentils
2 teaspoons Dijon mustard
1 red onion, peeled and chopped
½ cup semi-dried tomatoes, chopped
2 sprigs of thyme, leaves only, chopped
zest and juice of 2 lemons
3 tablespoons extra virgin olive oil
salt and freshly ground black pepper

a small bunch of flatleaf parsley, chopped

For the halibut
2 tablespoons olive oil
2 boneless halibut fillets, weighing 5½–6 ounces each
juice of ½ lemon
2 tablespoons pesto or chermoula sauce (see page 48), to serve

1 For the ragù, pour the lentils into a small saucepan. Place on low heat and add the Dijon mustard, red onion, semi-dried tomatoes (including their juices), thyme, lemon zest and juice, and the olive oil. Season with salt and pepper and heat for 5 to 6 minutes to let all the flavors infuse. Once the ragù is warmed through, remove it from the heat and add the chopped parsley. Let cool.

2 Now you can cook the fish. Heat the olive oil in a skillet and add the fish, skin-side down. Season the fish on the flesh side, reduce the heat, and cook until the underside is golden brown, about 8 minutes (depending on the thickness of the fish). Then turn the fish over and pour in the lemon juice. Turn the heat off and let the residual heat in the pan finish off the cooking. The fish can also be broiled or grilled if you prefer (cook for 4 to 5 minutes on each side).

3 When the fish has cooked through and you are ready to serve, place a large spoonful of the cooled lentil ragù onto each plate. Lay the fish over the ragù and top with a spoonful of pesto or chermoula sauce.

If you don't like fish, try this dish with a plump chicken breast. Cook the chicken on the skin side to ensure a lovely crispy finish.

SIRLOIN STEAK WITH BLUE CHEESE BUTTER

25

TOTAL

Preparation 15

Cooking 10

plus 5 minutes

resting time

Serves 2

The best things in life are often the simplest! Need I say more?

For the blue cheese butter
⅓ cup unsalted butter, cut into cubes
**2¾ ounces good strong blue cheese like
    a Stilton or Roquefort**
zest of 1 lemon
2 tablespoons chopped parsley
salt and freshly ground black pepper

For the steaks
2 good-quality boneless top sirloin steaks,
**weighing about 7–9 ounces each (aged
    for at least 28 days if possible)**
2 tablespoons olive oil

To serve
a bunch of watercress
juice of 1 lemon
2 tablespoons olive oil
**baked potatoes or Chunky Potato Wedges,
    see page 123 (optional)**

1 First make the butter. Place all the butter, except for two cubes, in a blender along with the blue cheese, lemon zest, and parsley. Season with pepper and blend until everything is combined. Transfer the contents into a bowl and set aside.

2 Season the steaks on both sides. Pour the olive oil into a hot skillet and lay in the steaks. Don't move the steaks around too much. A 1¼-inch-thick steak will need around 5 minutes per side for the steak to be cooked medium. Once the steak has had its first 5 minutes, drop in the remaining cubes of butter and turn the steak. You should see lots of caramelization—this is very important for the flavor of the finished dish.

3 While the steaks are cooking, make sure you keep spooning the butter in the pan over them so they stay nice and juicy. When cooked, take them out of the pan and let rest for at least 5 minutes. If you don't do this, all the work will be for nothing and your steaks will be tough.

4 To serve, place the steaks on your serving plates and add a big spoonful of the blue cheese butter. Dress the watercress leaves with the lemon juice and olive oil and serve on the side together with either a baked potato or the Chunky Potato Wedges, if you wish.

**This dish is
great followed
by a Tiramisu
(see page 162).**

WHITE CRAB AND GREEN APPLE COCKTAIL WITH AVOCADO AND LIME PURÉE

15
TOTAL

Preparation 15
Cooking 0
Serves 4

This is a really elegant little appetizer, lovely and light and ideal for entertaining in summer. You can serve it a few ways, either as a little canapé on toasted bruschetta, or in a cocktail glass for a more robust dish. I thinks it's great both ways, and if you only served this to me, I'd be very happy indeed.

For the crab and apple cocktail
2 Granny Smith apples, skin left on and
   grated or cut into thin matchsticks
14 ounces cooked lump crabmeat
1 tablespoon sour cream
½ small bunch of chives, snipped
a small handful of basil leaves, chopped
zest and juice of 2 limes

For the avocado and lime purée
2 avocados

zest and juice of 1 lime
1 small red chile, seeded and chopped
2 tablespoons sour cream
salt and freshly ground black pepper
olive oil (optional)

To serve
2 Boston lettuces, finely sliced
1 lime
chives or chervil, to garnish (optional)

Serve as an appetizer before the Sirloin Steak with Blue Cheese Butter (see page 88) or the Clams and Smoky Bacon (see page 97).

1 As soon as you have grated the apples, put all the crab and apple cocktail ingredients into a bowl and mix together with a wooden spoon to stop the apples from browning.

2 Place all the ingredients for the avocado purée into a food processor and season with salt and pepper. Blend thoroughly—if the mixture gets a bit stuck, add some olive oil to help it on its way. It should be as smooth as possible.

3 If you are serving this in glasses, put a small amount of the sliced lettuce at the bottom of each one along with a squeeze of lime juice. Spoon 2 to 3 tablespoons of the avocado purée on top and then evenly distribute the crab mix. Garnish with chives or some chervil, if available.

SEARED DUCK BREAST WITH WATERCRESS, CASHEWS, AND POMEGRANATE

30

TOTAL

Preparation 10

Cooking 20

Serves 4

or 6 to 8 as an appetizer

This light dish is best served at room temperature and therefore perfect for a summer evening. It takes hardly any time to prepare and the only thing that actually needs cooking is the duck.

For the dressing
zest of 2 oranges
juice of 1 lemon
6 tablespoons olive oil
a pinch of ground cinnamon
a pinch of ground cumin
1 teaspoon balsamic vinegar
1 tablespoon Dijon mustard

1 teaspoon honey

For the duck
4 duck breasts, skin on
¾ cup cashew nuts
heaping ¾ cup pomegranate seeds
10½ ounces watercress, big stems
removed

1 Preheat the oven to 350°F. To make the dressing, place all the ingredients into a glass jar, tightly screw on the lid, and shake hard until all the ingredients have combined. Set the 2 zested oranges aside for the duck.

2 Make four or five light slashes in the fat of the duck. Rub 2 tablespoons of dressing from the jar into the duck breasts. Place an ovenproof skillet on the stove, turn on the heat to medium, and lay in the duck breasts. It's better to start cooking the duck in a cold pan so that the fat can melt and the marinade won't burn. Cook the duck, skin-side down, for 6 to 8 minutes. Keep checking that the marinade isn't catching.

3 While the duck is cooking, cut off the top and bottom of the zested oranges. Using a small serrated knife, remove the outer peel and pith. Cut the segments from the orange by holding it in your hand, cutting in between each membrane, and pushing out the juicy segment. Let the segments fall into a clean bowl. Squeeze out any remaining juice into the duck pan.

4 Turn the duck over and finish cooking in the oven for an additional 5 minutes for pink meat and 10 minutes for well done. Remove from the oven and let rest.

5 Spread the cashew nuts over a baking sheet and toast in the oven for 5 minutes, or until golden brown.

When blood oranges are in season, use them if possible.

6 Mix the pomegranate seeds with the orange segments. Pour over half the dressing, mix in the cashews and watercress, and pile high on plates or a large platter. Slice the duck and place on top of the salad. Drizzle over the remaining dressing and serve.

BAKED SKATE WING WITH ROASTED ARTICHOKES, OLIVES, AND CAPERS

25

TOTAL

Preparation 10
Cooking 15
Serves 4

Try the roasted artichokes, capers, and olives with some boiled baby new potatoes to make a great side dish to go with chicken or pork.

Skate is a highly underused fish that has great texture and is extremely easy to cook. I find that it is also a really good choice of fish to introduce to nonfish lovers. Unlike other fish, it has big cartilage-type bones that the meat pulls away from with ease. This is an all-in-one-pan dish, so there's not too much cleanup and hardly any preparation needed. What could be better?

**4 skate wings, weighing about
  4½–6 ounces each
1½ cups (10½ ounces) marinated
  artichokes, drained (roasted ones in oil)
3 tablespoons black olives
salt and freshly ground black pepper
2 tablespoons olive oil**

**3 tablespoons butter
⅓ cup plus 1 tablespoon white wine
4 tablespoons capers in vinegar**

To serve
**2 tablespoons chopped parsley
boiled new potatoes**

1 Preheat the oven to 400°F. Lay the skate wings in a shallow roasting pan (you may need to divide the ingredients between two pans depending on the size of the wings). Scatter over the artichokes and olives. Season with a few pinches of salt and lots of black pepper. Drizzle over the olive oil, dot the butter over the fish, and pour over the white wine.

2 Put the pan in the oven for 10 minutes, then remove and scatter over the capers. Return to the oven for an additional 5 minutes.

3 Remove the pan from the oven and sprinkle over the chopped parsley. Serve at the table with some new potatoes.

CLAMS AND SMOKY BACON

25
TOTAL

Preparation 10
Cooking 15
Serves 2
or 4 as an appetizer

Try seving with the White Crab and Green Apple Cocktail to start (see page 91), or follow with the Almond, Hazelnut and Vanilla Cookies (see page 147).

This is the perfect quick dinner for a special night. I know clams are easy to come by in most supermarkets now, but I still get really excited about cooking them. They will always remind me of family holidays to the South of France when I was little and I would spend hours picking the lovely juicy meat out of the tiny shells. My top tip is to always buy more clams than you think you're going to eat because, trust me, you'll want to go back for more.

2 tablespoons olive oil
5½ ounces smoked bacon slices or smoked pancetta, chopped into fine strips
2 shallots, peeled and chopped
¼ teaspoon dried red pepper flakes
1 bay leaf
2 garlic cloves, peeled and chopped
4 tablespoons butter

½ cup heavy cream
4½ pounds small live clams, cleaned
½ cup Vermouth or dry white wine
freshly ground black pepper

To serve
1 lemon, cut into wedges
extra virgin olive oil, to drizzle
crusty bread

1 Heat the oil in a large saucepan and add the bacon, shallots, red pepper flakes, and bay leaf. Cook them gently until soft, 4 to 5 minutes, then add the garlic and the butter. Let the butter melt before adding the cream.

2 Increase the heat, bring to a boil, and boil the cream for 2 minutes, then add the clams and Vermouth or white wine. Season well with pepper, stir, and put on a tight-fitting lid.

3 Let the clams cook for 5 minutes, shaking the pan hard halfway through. Once all the clams are open, serve straight away with a wedge of lemon, a drizzle of olive oil, and a big chunk of crusty bread to soak up all the juices.

RED WINE, GORGONZOLA, AND ORANGE RISOTTO

30
TOTAL

Preparation 10
Cooking 20
Serves 4
or 6 to 8 as an
appetizer

It's not often that I make risotto, but when I do I need it to be interesting, so I like to bulk out the rice with a full-bodied red wine, nuts, and a tasty strong cheese. There's always a different flavor in each mouthful. This is my favorite risotto so far—it's simple yet so full of flavor and also works well as an appetizer.

1½ quarts chicken or vegetable stock
2 tablespoons olive oil
⅓ cup butter
2 shallots, peeled and chopped
1¾ cups risotto rice
¾ cup plus 1 tablespoon red wine

salt and freshly ground black pepper
zest of 2 oranges
7 ounces Gorgonzola
1 cup grated Parmesan cheese, plus extra
    shavings to serve (optional)
1 cup crushed walnuts (optional)

1 Place the stock in a saucepan and bring to a boil.

2 Place a large shallow saucepan on the stove and turn the heat to medium. Add the olive oil and half the butter. When the butter has melted, add the shallots and cook until soft, 3 minutes. Add the rice and stir around in the butter and oil until all the grains are coated.

3 Increase the heat to full and add the red wine. Stir the grains around in the wine continuously until all the wine has been absorbed. Then start gradually adding the stock, a ladleful at a time. Never stop gently stirring the risotto. Once one ladleful of stock has been absorbed, add the next. Season with a big pinch of salt and pepper.

4 When the rice is nearly cooked (after about 14 minutes of stirring), add the orange zest. Add another ladle of stock, then crumble in the Gorgonzola and stir well so that all the cheese melts. Taste for seasoning—you will quite likely need more pepper.

5 When the rice is cooked to al dente, add the remaining butter and the Parmesan cheese. Stir through and serve scattered with Parmesan shavings and the crushed walnuts, if you wish.

A full-bodied red wine works best for this risotto, so buy the strongest you can to get maximum flavor.

ROASTED QUAIL AND FIGS STUFFED WITH GOAT CHEESE AND HONEY WITH A PICKLED WALNUT DRESSING

⏱

35

TOTAL

Preparation 10
Cooking 25
Serves 2
or 4 as an appetizer

I can't help but buy quails when I see them, and I've never had a displeased diner when I've cooked up this appetizer for them. It's quite big and, of course, can also be eaten as an entrée, but I tend to go with a light main if I cook this at a dinner party. Serve quails slightly pink and they go particularly well with the sweet/salty duo of goat cheese and fig. They are easy to prepare and, as they are so small, this dish cooks in no time.

6 large ripe figs
7 ounces goat cheese
4 whole quails
salt and freshly ground black pepper
olive oil, for roasting
2 tablespoons honey
corn salad or pea shoots, to serve

For the pickled walnut dressing
6 pickled walnuts, coarsely chopped
1 tablespoon Dijon mustard
2 tablespoons sticky balsamic vinegar
1 tablespoon chopped parsley
4 tablespoons olive oil

1 Preheat the oven to 400°F. Cut the figs crisscross style from the top to halfway down and push up from the bottom to open them out like a flower. Push as much goat cheese into the opening of the fig as you can—be very generous.

2 Season the quails with salt and pepper and place on a baking sheet along with the figs. Drizzle both the quails and the figs with the olive oil and the honey and put in the oven to roast for 12 to 15 minutes.

3 Meanwhile, make a dressing by mixing the pickled walnuts with the mustard, vinegar, chopped parsley, and olive oil.

4 After 15 minutes, remove the baking sheet from the oven, take out the figs, and set aside. Return the quails to the oven for an additional 10 minutes.

5 Serve 1 quail and 1 fig per person, garnish with a handful of corn salad or pea shoots, and drizzle with the pickled walnut dressing. You can carve the meat from the quail for presentation purposes if you prefer by removing both the legs, cutting down the breastbone, and removing both breasts.

Most game goes really with figs—try this dish with a pan-fried pigeon breast.

PAN-FRIED MONKFISH WITH WILD MUSHROOMS, CARAMELIZED ONIONS, AND A HERBY SOUR CREAM SAUCE

Monkfish is a really meaty fish that holds up well to big bold flavors. It's a great fish to serve to nonfish-loving guests and is also very easy and forgiving to cook. It won't fall apart like some fish but you can of course overcook it, so be careful to cook gently until perfectly cooked through. Mushrooms are my number one choice of accompaniment with sweet onions.

For the onions
2 tablespoons butter
1 tablespoon olive oil
3 large onions, peeled and finely sliced
⅓ cup plus 1 tablespoon white wine
1 tablespoon white sugar
1 tablespoon white wine vinegar

For the monkfish
4 tablespoons butter
2 garlic cloves, peeled and chopped

4 sprigs of thyme, leaves only
2 monkfish fillets, weighing about
    5½ ounces each
⅓ cup plus 1 tablespoon white wine
9 ounces wild mushrooms or a package of
    mixed mushrooms, the large ones sliced
a bunch of flatleaf parsley, chopped
1 lemon, cut in half
salt and freshly ground black pepper
⅓ cup plus 1 tablespoon sour cream

1 To caramelize the onions, heat the butter and oil in a saucepan, add the onions, and gently sauté for 5 to 6 minutes. Add the white wine, sugar, and vinegar and cook until all the liquid has evaporated and the onions are soft and sweet, 10 to 15 minutes. Keep them moving in the pan to ensure they don't burn.

2 Meanwhile, heat up a large skillet and add the butter, garlic, and thyme leaves. Add the monkfish and color for about 2 minutes on each side until golden. Add a drop of oil if the butter starts to burn. Cook for an additional 2 minutes, then add the wine and cook for 3 more minutes.

3 Move the monkfish to one side, add the mushrooms, and cook until they are wilted, 2 to 3 minutes. Add half the parsley, the juice of half the lemon, a big pinch of salt, and lots of black pepper. Meanwhile, make the herby sour cream sauce by heating the sour cream in a small saucepan with the remaining parsley and the juice of the other half of the lemon.

4 Serve the onions with the fish and the mushrooms. You can serve the sour cream sauce on the side or on top of the fish.

30
TOTAL

Preparation 10
Cooking 20
Serves 2

Any meaty fish works well with this recipe— halibut is great. For something completely different, try using veal.

CRAB LINGUINE

This is simply the most satisfying quick dish that I can think of. I absolutely love crab, and although it is quite expensive, it is such a special product that should be treated with the utmost respect. Crab speaks for itself, so needs very little doing to it.

salt
18 ounces dry linguine
3 tablespoons olive oil
1 shallot, peeled and finely diced
2 red peppers, seeded and finely chopped
a pinch of dried red pepper flakes
3 garlic cloves, peeled and sliced

½ cup white wine
⅓ cup butter
16 to 20 cherry tomatoes, halved
juice of 1 large lemon
12 ounces cooked lump crabmeat
½ bunch of flatleaf parsley, finely chopped

1 Put a big pot of water on the stove to boil and add a pinch of salt. When the water starts to boil, add the pasta and cook as directed on the package until al dente.

2 In a separate pan, pour in the olive oil and turn to medium heat. Add the shallot, chiles, red pepper flakes, and garlic. Cook gently for a few minutes in the olive oil (make sure the garlic does not burn). Add the white wine and the butter and bring to a boil to burn off the alcohol. Add the cherry tomatoes, lemon juice, and crabmeat.

3 Once the pasta is cooked, drain, reserving a couple of tablespoons of the pot liquor. Mix the pasta into the crab sauce along with the reserved liquid. Stir through the parsley and serve.

25
TOTAL

Preparation 10
Cooking 15
Serves 4

As this is so quick to make, why not spend another few minutes making Blueberry Pie for dessert (see page 152)?

COD AND PAPRIKA CHOWDER

45
TOTAL

Preparation 15
Cooking 30
Serves 4
as a light
main course

A chowder is a lovely thick soup that works well as an appetizer or main course. My recipe for chowder is quite meaty, so I tend to serve it as an entrée, but a nice alternative is to omit the fish and make the dish a bit lighter. The base to a good chowder is very important, so follow the recipe closely and it will be fabulous.

2 cups plus 1 tablespoon low-fat milk
1 fish bouillon cube
1¼ pounds cod fillet, skinned
1 bay leaf
scant ½ cup butter
scant 1 cup diced smoked pancetta
1 leek, trimmed and white part finely diced
10½ ounces butternut squash, peeled and
    finely diced into ½-inch pieces

2 garlic cloves, peeled and chopped
1 teaspoon smoked paprika
⅓ cup Vermouth or white wine
3 tablespoons all-purpose flour
1 x 7-ounce can corn kernels
1 tablespoon chopped parsley
juice of 1 lemon
freshly ground black pepper
crackers, to serve (optional)

1 Put the milk into a large saucepan, crumble in the bouillon cube, and add the fish and bay leaf. Turn the heat to medium and bring the milk to a simmer. Remove from the heat, carefully lift out the fish onto a plate, and set aside the pot liquor for later.

2 Melt half the butter in another saucepan on medium heat and add the pancetta. Cook for a few minutes before adding the leek, butternut squash, garlic, and smoked paprika. Soften for a few minutes before adding the Vermouth or white wine. Cook for about 10 minutes until all the ingredients are tender, then remove everything from the pan and set aside.

3 Melt the remaining butter in the same pan. Add the flour and mix to form a paste. Cook for 3 minutes, always moving the paste around in the pan, and then gradually add the reserved pot liquor from the fish in three or four batches. Mix continuously to remove any floury lumps. Let the mix boil in between adding the next batch of liquid. If the soup looks too thick (it should be the consistency of runny yogurt), stir in a small amount of water.

4 Flake the cod into the chowder, leaving it as chunky as possible, and then add the cooked vegetables, corn, and any juices. Stir in the parsley and season with lemon juice and pepper. Crumble over some crackers, if you like.

**Try using
smoked cod as
an alternative.**

FRIED SQUID WITH CHORIZO, FETA, AND CHICKPEA SALAD

25
TOTAL

Preparation 15
Cooking 10
Serves 2

or 4 as an appetizer

Squid is one of those ingredients that needs to be either cooked quickly or long and slowly. I personally prefer the quick method, as I tend to be quite impatient, which makes this the ideal meal to cook after coming home from work when you need something pronto.

For the salad
1 x 14-ounce can chickpeas (garbanzo beans)
½ cup pitted black olives, coarsely chopped
2 garlic cloves, peeled and finely grated
1 red onion, trimmed and thinly sliced
a small bunch of flatleaf parsley, chopped
⅔ cup crumbled feta
1 tablespoon sherry vinegar
2 tablespoons olive oil
salt and freshly ground black pepper

3½ ounces arugula

For the squid
12 cleaned squid tubes
2 teaspoons olive oil
5½ ounces chorizo, cut into slices
1 teaspoon smoked paprika
juice of 1 lemon
a sprig of oregano, leaves only, finely chopped
crusty bread, to serve

1 To make the chickpea salad, drain the chickpeas (garbanzo beans) and place in a large mixing bowl. Add the olives, garlic, onion, and parsley. Add the feta and mix well. Pour over the sherry vinegar and olive oil and season with salt and pepper.

2 To prepare the squid, slit the cleaned tubes in half so that they open out like a book. Gently score the inside of the flesh in a crisscross pattern with a sharp knife, then cut into three pieces. This will help the squid cook more quickly and make it more tender.

3 Heat up a skillet, add the olive oil, and let it get hot. Add the chorizo to the pan and cook until the fat runs, 3 to 4 minutes. When that starts to happen, increase the heat and add the squid along with the smoked paprika. Cook for 3 to 4 minutes, then add the lemon juice, salt and pepper, and the oregano.

4 Pour the cooked squid and chorizo into the salad and mix in the arugula. Serve with crusty bread.

This dish also makes a great appetizer followed by Sirloin Steak with Blue Cheese Butter (see page 88).

SEARED TUNA WITH GRAPEFRUIT, PEPPER, AND BASIL SALSA

This recipe makes a great light main course and creates very little mess and stress. I've also served this as an appetizer before a heavy entrée when I serve three or four slices of the rare seared tuna and a spoonful of the salsa. It's light, healthy, and very refreshing.

cracked black pepper and salt
2 x 4½-ounce tuna steaks
olive oil, to drizzle

For the salsa
1 whole grapefruit
3 large plum tomatoes

6 scallions
1 large red pepper, seeds in, finely chopped
salt and freshly ground black pepper
a pinch of white sugar
zest and juice of 1 lime
2 tablespoons extra virgin olive oil
a handful of basil leaves

1 Make the salsa by segmenting the grapefruit and cutting the segments into four pieces. Cut the tomatoes into quarters and remove all the seeds and pulp. Now cut each petal into four strips and mix with the grapefruit. Finely slice the scallions, including the green part, and add to the salsa mixture. Mix in the red chile, leaving the seeds in for a bit of a kick if you like. Season with salt, pepper, and the sugar and add the lime juice and zest along with a couple of tablespoons of olive oil. (Let the salsa stand overnight if you have time.)

2 Heat a skillet or grill pan until it starts to smoke. Season the tuna steaks with salt and pepper and rub with a little oil. Lay the fish into the hot pan and sear for 1 to 2 minutes on each side, depending on how you like it cooked. Remove from the pan and let cool.

3 Once the tuna is rested, cut it into four or five thin slices. Add the basil leaves to the salsa—either coarsely tear them or leave whole if they are small. Serve the fish with a big spoonful of the salsa on the side.

25

TOTAL

Preparation 20
Cooking 5
Serves 2

Try following with The Dreaded Soufflé for dessert (see page 150).

SEA BASS WITH A FENNEL, ORANGE, PINE NUT, AND GOLDEN RAISIN SALAD

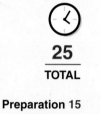

25
TOTAL

Preparation 15
Cooking 10
Serves 4

If you're craving something sweet, try the Berry Gratin (see page 148) to finish.

This is surprisingly fast to prepare and looks colorful and interesting on the plate, so is guaranteed to impress. It's got a very Mediterranean feel and is ideal for a summer's eve or as a light main course after a larger appetizer.

2 large oranges
½ cup golden raisins
4 fennel bulbs, trimmed and very finely sliced
⅔ cup toasted pine nuts (blanched whole almonds are also good)

a small bunch of dill weed, coarsely chopped
juice of 2 lemons
1 tablespoon extra virgin olive oil
salt and freshly ground black pepper
1 tablespoon vegetable oil
4 large sea bass fillets, pin-boned

1 Cut the top and bottom off the oranges and remove all the outer skin and pith using a small serrated knife. Remove the orange segments and put them into a large mixing bowl. Pour any juice caught in the bowl into a small saucepan, add the golden raisins, and place on very low heat until the juice boils. Remove from the heat and let cool.

2 Add the fennel, pine nuts, and dill to the orange segments. Pour over the cooled golden raisins and orange juice, half the lemon juice, and the olive oil. Season to taste.

3 Put a skillet on medium heat and add the vegetable oil. Season the fish and, when the oil is hot, lay the fillets, skin-side down, in the pan. Cook for 3 to 4 minutes before turning the fish over and pouring over half the remaining lemon juice. Turn off the heat and let the fish finish cooking in the residual heat for an additional 3 minutes. Serve straight away with the crispy fennel salad.

VEAL CHOP WITH MUSTARD MASH AND A MADEIRA AND MUSHROOM SAUCE

35

TOTAL

Preparation 15
Cooking 20
Serves 2

I just love veal, and if you're a sensible shopper and choose veal that has been reared in a humane way, eating it is absolutely fine. It goes so well with this mustard mash and the Madeira sauce is a must.

3 large potatoes, peeled and cut into
  1¼-inch chunks
2 garlic cloves, peeled and left whole
salt and freshly ground black pepper
5 tablespoons heavy cream
scant ½ cup butter
1 tablespoon whole-grain mustard
1 tablespoon olive oil
2 veal chops on the bone

For the Madeira and mushroom sauce
2⅔ cups sliced crimini mushrooms
  (or wild mushrooms if they are in season)
2 tablespoons butter
2 sprigs of thyme, leaves only
⅓ cup plus 1 tablespoon Madeira wine
⅓ cup plus 1 tablespoon heavy cream
juice of ½ lemon

1 Put the potatoes into a saucepan and cover with water, then add the garlic and a big pinch of salt and bring to a boil. Cook until tender, about 20 minutes, and then drain. Heat the cream with ⅓ cup of the butter in a small saucepan and mash the potatoes really well. Gradually add the hot cream and butter to the mashed potatoes, mix in the mustard, and season well.

2 While the potatoes are cooking, heat a large skillet with the olive oil and remaining butter. Season the chops on both sides with salt and pepper and lay into the oil. Cook for 6 to 7 minutes on each side (depending on the thickness) until golden brown. The chops should be served pink. Keep spooning the pan drippings over them as they cook to keep them moist. When cooked, remove from the pan and let rest.

3 To make the sauce, add the mushrooms to the pan along with the butter and thyme. Sauté for 1 minute before adding the Madeira wine and cream. Bring to a boil, season with salt and pepper, and add the lemon juice.

4 Serve the mustard mash with the chop on the side and a good spoonful of the mushroom sauce.

To make a really smooth mash, I like to use a ricer— this is the best way I know to ensure there are no lumps.

Tuck In

Not every night has to be a sit-down dinner. One of the best ways to enjoy food and the company of others is by laying out a big spread and letting everyone tuck in. You might be celebrating or catching up with friends, having the family over, and don't have enough chairs for everyone to sit on, or just want something really informal where everyone can feel relaxed. My favorite is a night with the girls where we can all really eat our fill, but I know many moms, wives, and girlfriends who will cook this type of food for the kids after school or as a quick snack for the other important people in their lives. Dinners don't always have to be eaten with a knife and fork sitting around a perfectly laid table. This is good, wholesome food that can be set out ready for people to pick from, making your life a whole lot simpler.

HOMEMADE CHICKEN AND HALLOUMI SHISH

30

TOTAL

Preparation 15
Cooking 15
plus marinating time

Serves 4

I regularly feed this to friends after a night out or when I wasn't expecting company, as I tend to have all the basics stored in my fridge most of the time. Don't even think about making this dish unless you have a hot chili sauce in your pantry—it's just not the same without it.

15 mini chicken cutlets
1 x 7-ounce block halloumi cheese or
   queso fresco, cut into 12 cubes
1 lemon, cut into wedges

For the marinade
1 red pepper finely chopped
2 garlic cloves, peeled and grated or
   finely chopped
grated zest and juice of 1 lemon
4 tablespoons olive oil
1 tablespoon ground cumin
1 teaspoon ground coriander

salt and freshly ground black pepper

For the pitas
4 large pita breads
½ small white cabbage, shredded
1 red onion, peeled and finely sliced
2 large plum tomatoes, sliced
¼ cucumber, sliced
heaping ¾ cup hummus
4 tablespoons Greek-style yogurt
4 large pickled chiles (not too hot)
½ bunch of cilantro
hot chili sauce, to serve

1 Put the chicken and halloumi or queso fresco into a large mixing bowl and add the marinade ingredients. Cover and set aside to marinate.

2 Preheat the broiler or grill to hot or heat a grill pan. Skewer the chicken and the cheese onto metal skewers or wooden ones that have been soaked in water for a few minutes to stop them burning. You should have three pieces of cheese on each.

3 Lay the skewers under the broiler or on the grill or grill pan and cook for 6 minutes. Turn the skewers over and cook for an additional 6 minutes. Squeeze over the juice of quarter of a lemon.

4 Heat up the pitas either in a toaster or under the broiler. Cut down the middle of the pita with a sharp knife and make a pocket. Pull the chicken and halloumi off the skewers into a bowl. Have the salad ingredients laid out in front of you.

5 Spread the inside of the pitas generously with hummus before loading in the salad, more lemon juice, and finally the chicken and cheese. Spoon a dollop of yogurt on each pita, then lay across a chile, tear over some cilantro, and serve with a good dollop of hot chili sauce.

If you are serving these to bigger numbers, you could put all the salad and accompaniments in the middle of the table and let your guests build their skewers themselves.

ROSIE'S VEGAN CURRY (THE BOYS NEVER KNEW!)

45–50
TOTAL

Preparation 10
Cooking 35–40
Serves 6 to 8

My wonderful cousin Rosie recently became a vegan. A horrible thought for us meat lovers, but an exciting challenge for a chef like me to have to come up with a recipe to not only serve to her but also my boyfriend and his meat-loving friends who had just returned from a bad soccer game and would need some serious cheering up with a decent hearty meal.

2 tablespoons vegetable oil
2 large onions, peeled and finely chopped
3 large green peppers, chopped
2-inch piece of fresh ginger, peeled and finely chopped
4 garlic cloves, peeled and finely chopped
3 teaspoons ground cumin
2 teaspoons ground coriander
2 teaspoons chili powder
2 teaspoons turmeric
2 tablespoons tomato paste
salt
1 cinnamon stick
2 x 14-ounce cans diced tomatoes

2 x 14-ounce cans green lentils, drained
1 butternut squash, cut into ¾-inch dice (no need to peel, just remove the seeds)
1 cauliflower, cut into small florets
3 green beans, trimmed and cut into thirds
a large bunch of cilantro, coarsely chopped
juice of 1 lemon

To serve
rice or naan and plain yogurt or raita

1 Heat a heavy-bottomed pan on medium heat. Add the oil to the pan and the onions, chiles, ginger, and garlic. Cook until the onions start to soften and go translucent, 4 to 5 minutes.

2 Add all the dried spices and stir to coat the onion mixture well. Cook for an additional 4 to 5 minutes before adding the tomato paste, a good pinch of salt, and the cinnamon stick. Stir well. Add the canned tomatoes and lentils, reduce the heat, and let the sauce simmer for 10 minutes.

3 Add the vegetables, starting with those that take longer to cook. First add the butternut squash and cook for 10 to 15 minutes, then add the cauliflower and cook for an additional 15 to 20 minutes. Add about ½ cup water at this stage if the stew is looking a little dry.

4 Just before serving, bring the curry to a boil, add the green beans, and cook until just tender. Then add the cilantro. Taste for seasoning and add the lemon juice. Stir well before serving with either rice or naan and plain yogurt or raita on the side.

To make sure this meal is vegan-friendly, use soy yogurt to serve.

BARBECUE CHINESE RIBS

40

TOTAL

Preparation 10

Cooking 30

Serves 8

We all love barbecued ribs and this is a great recipe that can also be used on chicken. You don't have to marinate the meat, as it's a thick sauce and will stick and caramelize as the meat cooks. This really is great finger food for a relaxed evening.

2 red peppers, finely chopped
1-inch piece of fresh ginger, peeled and
    finely chopped
3 garlic cloves, peeled and finely chopped
⅓ cup plus 1 tablespoon soy sauce
3 tablespoons honey
2 tablespoons dark brown sugar
2 tablespoons tomato paste
3 tablespoons ketchup

1 tablespoon red wine vinegar
2 tablespoons vegetable oil
a large pinch of salt
20 pork ribs

To serve
1 red pepper, sliced
2 scallions, trimmed and sliced

1 Preheat the oven to 350°F. Make the marinade by combining all the ingredients, except for the pork ribs, in a food processor. Blend to a fine paste.

2 Pour half the sauce over the ribs in a shallow ovenproof container and rub in well. Put in the oven and cook the pork ribs for 30 minutes (or 25 minutes if using chicken wings). Check regularly to see if the sauce is burning a bit too much or drying out—if this happens, pour in a couple of tablespoons of water.

3 Pour the remaining sauce into a saucepan and boil for 3 to 4 minutes to heat the sauce for dipping the ribs. Remove the pan from the heat and set aside.

4 Once the meat is cooked, transfer the ribs to a cutting board. Use a sharp knife to cut in between each rib to carve them into individual portions. If you wish you can transfer to plates, spoon over the sauce, and sprinkle the chile and scallions on top. This dish is perfect with some sticky rice on the side.

This marinade has many uses—it's great just as a dip or smothered over chicken wings.

BREADED SHRIMP AND TARTAR SAUCE

35

TOTAL

Preparation 20
Cooking 15
Serves 8

I love the sort of food you can carry through in a basket and let everyone dig into. No ceremony here, ladies and gentlemen! Just pick it up, dunk it, and enjoy. Watch out, though... they'll be hot!

For the tartar sauce
2 eggs, separated
1 teaspoon Dijon mustard
1¼ ups vegetable oil
salt and freshly ground black pepper
juice of ½ lemon
2 teaspoons capers
1 tablespoon baby gherkins

For the scampi
1 quart vegetable oil, for deep-frying (optional)
heaping ¾ cup all-purpose flour
2 large eggs
2 cups dry bread crumbs
30 large raw shrimp, peeled and deveined
2 lemons, cut into wedges, to serve

1 If you plan to cook your shrimp in the oven, preheat it to 400°F. First make the tartar sauce. Put the egg yolks into a blender or a bowl with the Dijon mustard (reserve the egg whites for the shrimp). Beat or blend together well before very slowly adding the oil, drop by drop. You can speed up the process once the mixture starts to thicken. Once thickened to the consistency of mayonnaise, season with salt and pepper and add the lemon juice. Blend in the capers and gherkins so that they are small but still chunky. Chop them by hand and mix in if you're not using a blender.

2 If you are deep-frying your shrimp, put the oil in a deep fryer or a wide, deep pan and fill no more than halfway. Turn the heat to medium.

3 Put the flour, whole eggs and egg whites, and the bread crumbs into three separate bowls. Beat the eggs together and season the flour. Pat the shrimp dry and pass first through the flour, then the egg, and then the bread crumbs. Coat well.

4 If cooking in the oven, put the breaded shrimp right onto a baking sheet and bake for 10 to 15 minutes until golden brown. Turn them once during cooking.

5 If deep-frying, check the oil temperature by dropping in a pinch of bread crumbs. If they sizzle and rise to the top, the oil is ready. Cook the shrimp in batches of about five or six at a time. Place the shrimp onto a large slotted spoon and gently lower into the oil. Move them around until they are golden brown, about 2 to 4 minutes. Remove from the oil and lay on paper towels to drain while you cook the rest.

6 Season with salt and serve with wedges of lemon and the tartar sauce.

For a night of nibbles, serve alongside the Deep-fried Mozzarella Balls with Jalapeño Cheese Dip (see page 134).

LEMONGRASS STEAMED SHRIMP

25–26
TOTAL

Preparation 20
Cooking 5–6
Serves 4

If you are
serving this
dish as a main
course, steam
some jasmine
rice and serve
it on the side.

This is a traditional way of cooking shrimp in Thailand, a place very close to my heart and one of my favorite methods of cooking. Your dinner will be packed full of flavor as well as looking very pretty on the plate or platter. This recipe is ideal for finger food at a little party or gathering, or as a nice light entrée at a dinner party.

24 raw large shrimp, peeled and deveined
4 sticks of lemongrass, first 2 layers peeled
  off to make the stick into a spear
2-inch piece of fresh ginger, peeled and
  cut into fine strips
½ green pepper, finely sliced
2 tablespoons light soy sauce

1 teaspoon Thai fish sauce
juice of 1 lime
1 teaspoon superfine sugar
4 scallions, trimmed and sliced
Thai Dipping Sauce (see page 136), to
  serve (optional)

1 Bring a saucepan of water to a boil. I like to use a traditional bamboo steamer for this dish, although an upturned saucer in the bottom of a large, deep skillet that has a lid will also do as a makeshift steamer.

2 Spear as many of the shrimp onto the lemongrass spear as you can. If the shrimp are particularly big, you may need more than four lemongrass stalks.

3 Make the dressing by combining the ginger strips, chile, soy sauce, fish sauce, lime juice, and sugar in a bowl.

4 Place the shrimp skewers onto a plate that fits inside your steamer and pour over the dressing. Steam for 5 to 6 minutes until the shrimp have turned pink. Sprinkle with the sliced scallions and serve immediately with the Thai Dipping Sauce, if you like.

LAMB BURGERS AND CHUNKY POTATO WEDGES

45
TOTAL

Preparation 20
Cooking 25
Serves 6

Tell me a better thing to cook for a bunch of rowdy friends, family members, or kids? These burgers are big and meaty, but with a little fresh twist. A big toasted hamburger bun, juicy meat, and chunky wedges dipped and doused in mayo is really quite delicious and very indulgent—any friend would be highly impressed.

For the chunky wedges
6 large potatoes, skins left on, each cut
  into eight wedges
1 teaspoon ground cumin
1 teaspoon hot paprika
2 tablespoons olive oil
salt and freshly ground black pepper

For the burgers
1¾ pounds ground lamb
1 teaspoon ground cumin
½ bunch of cilantro, chopped

1 egg yolk
2 tablespoons vegetable oil
7 ounces mozzarella cheese
6 hamburger buns

To serve (optional)
3 large plum tomatoes, sliced
1 red onion, peeled and sliced
  into rings
6 large pickled gherkins, sliced
mayonnaise
ketchup

1 Preheat the oven to 375°F and the broiler to medium. Put the potato wedges in a bowl and mix with the cumin, paprika, oil, and salt and pepper. Lay them out evenly on a baking sheet and roast in the oven for about 25 minutes until they are golden and cooked through.

2 For the burgers, mix the lamb, cumin, cilantro, and egg yolk with some salt and pepper in a bowl. Divide the mixture into six, roll into balls, then flatten into patties.

3 Heat a large ovenproof skillet on high heat and add the vegetable oil. Lay in the burger patties and cook for 5 minutes on each side. Transfer the burgers to a cookie sheet, place a layer of torn mozzarella on each one, and put in the oven for 5 minutes.

4 Cut the hamburger buns in half and place under the broiler for 2 minutes while the burgers rest, or put them in the hot oven if you don't have a separate broiler. When they are slightly toasted, build the burgers with the tomatoes, onions, and gherkins, if using, and serve with the crispy potato wedges and loads of mayo and ketchup.

This also works really well with ground beef or even chicken—just make sure you cook it all the way through.

CHICKEN, APRICOT, AND CHICKPEA TAGINE

55
TOTAL

Preparation 15
Cooking 40
Serves 6

Tagine is the Moroccan word for the pot that their famous fruity casseroles are cooked in. Tagines have become very popular in many restaurants and homes, and this recipe is extremely easy and takes very little time and effort. I love meat and fruit served together and I think that more people should try it. This is the perfect dish when you have a full house, as it is cooked all in one pot and transfers straight from the oven to the table.

4 tablespoons vegetable oil
1¾ pounds chicken (or 10 boneless and skinless chicken thighs), diced into ¾-inch pieces
3 large onions, peeled and sliced
3 garlic cloves, peeled and chopped
1 teaspoon chopped fresh ginger
2 teaspoons ground cumin
1 teaspoon hot paprika
salt and freshly ground black pepper
1 cup dried apricots

2 x 14-ounce cans chickpeas (garbanzo beans), drained
2 x 14-ounce cans diced tomatoes
1 cup chicken stock
4 tablespoons honey
2 strips orange zest
6 to 8 tablespoons pitted black olives
a bunch of cilantro, torn
Pomegranate and Almond Couscous (see page 43), to serve (optional)

You can add diced potatoes to this dish to make it more substantial instead of serving it with couscous or rice. Add to the pan while the chicken is cooking and cook for 20 to 25 minutes until tender.

1 Heat a large casserole dish on medium heat and add half the oil. Pan-fry the pieces of chicken, in batches if necessary, until slightly golden, about 5 to 6 minutes. Remove from the pan and set aside.

2 Add the remaining oil to the pan and gently sauté the onions, garlic, and ginger until soft, 3 to 4 minutes. Add the cumin, hot paprika, and salt and pepper and stir well.

3 Return the chicken to the casserole and add the apricots, chickpeas (garbanzo beans), tomatoes, stock, honey, and the orange zest. Bring to the boil, then reduce the heat and let the casserole simmer for about 30 minutes. Add the olives during the last 10 minutes of cooking.

4 Scatter the tagine with the torn cilantro and serve with the Pomegrante and Almond Couscous alongside, if you like.

PORK AND PINEAPPLE SWEET AND SOUR NOODLE STIR-FRY

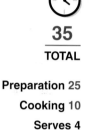

35
TOTAL

Preparation 25
Cooking 10
Serves 4

Sweet and sour is a takeout classic. This is a much healthier option that ticks everyone's boxes when having a relaxed night in. Stir-fries are instant cooking that make all our lives easier, so the more interesting we can make them, the better.

18 ounces pork cutlets, cut into
 ¾-inch pieces
6 tablespoons dark soy sauce
1 teaspoon sesame oil
1 tablespoon rice vinegar
4 teaspoons cornstarch
9 ounces dry cellophane or rice noodles or
 ready-cooked noodles
2 tablespoons peanut or vegetable oil
⅓ cup plus 1 tablespoon pineapple juice
1 tablespoon sweet chili sauce
a handful of cilantro, chopped
1 lime, cut into wedges

For the stir-fry
1-inch piece of fresh ginger, peeled and
 finely cut into strips
2 garlic cloves, peeled and finely chopped
2 red peppers, cut into slices
2 red bell peppers, seeded and cut into
 ¾-inch pieces
1 red onion, peeled and cut into
 ¾-inch pieces
6 scallions, trimmed and cut into
 1-inch pieces
1 x 8-ounce can pineapple chunks in juice
 or 1 whole pineapple, cut into chunks

1 Start by marinating the pork in 2 tablespoons of the soy sauce, the sesame oil, vinegar, and cornstarch. Let marinate while you prepare all the vegetables.

2 Soak the noodles in boiling water for 1 minute until soft. Drain and let soak in cold water until later. If you are using ready-cooked noodles, leave out this step.

3 Heat a wok or large skillet on the stove and add 1 tablespoon of the oil. Start cooking only when the wok is so hot that the oil is nearly smoking. Remove the pork from the marinade with a slotted spoon (reserve the marinade for later) and carefully put it into the hot wok. Stir-fry the pork until it is nearly cooked all the way through and you have a little color on the meat, about 2 minutes.

4 Remove the pork from the wok and add the remaining oil with the ginger, garlic, and chile. Stir-fry for 1 minute before adding the remaining vegetables and the pineapple. Cook for an additional 2 to 3 minutes before returning the pork to the wok along with the reserved pork marinade, the remaining 4 tablespoons soy sauce, the pineapple juice, and the sweet chili sauce. Boil the liquid in the bottom of the wok for 3 to 4 minutes, stirring continuously.

5 Fold in the prepared cellophane or rice noodles or ready-cooked noodles and scatter with the cilantro. Serve with a wedge of lime.

This also works well with jumbo shrimp or chicken.

MY CHOPPED SALAD

15

TOTAL

Preparation 15
Cooking 0
Serves 4 to 6

**Follow with
the Peach and
Pistachio Trifle
(see page 158).**

This is a salad that can be eaten as an appetizer or an entrée. But it is massive and I always make way too much. I love this dish because it is great at barbecues, when you have friends over, or just when you can't make up your mind so you go for a salad that literally contains everything. There's hardly any preparation involved, as most things come straight out of a package, which makes it doubly good!

⅔ cup (5½ ounces) semi-dried tomatoes
   (or chargrilled mixed vegetables),
   coarsely chopped
1 cup (7 ounces) marinated artichokes,
   quartered
8 cooked crispy bacon slices
3½ ounces blue cheese
2 cups cooked shredded chicken

1 cup coarsely chopped walnuts
1 x 14-ounce can corn kernels, drained
1 romaine lettuce, sliced
4 tablespoons crème fraîche or sour cream
1 tablespoon whole-grain mustard
juice of 1 lemon
salt and freshly ground black pepper
a large handful of basil leaves, to serve

1 Put the tomatoes and artichokes into a serving bowl. Break up the crispy bacon and crumble into the salad and then do the same with the cheese.

2 Add all the remaining ingredients and mix really well. Season with salt and pepper, then tear over the basil leaves to garnish. Serve immediately.

EASY CHEESY FONDUE

30

TOTAL

Preparation 10

Cooking 20

Serves 4 to 6

as a fun snack
with a few drinks

This is a dish to be cooked on a cold night in with a bunch of friends. I don't know anyone that wouldn't be tempted by a bowl of molten cheese and a variety of yummy stuff to dip in it. I've come up with a way that even if you don't have a fondue kit, you can still have a go at creating this Swiss culinary treat. Of course I've made a few changes, but all in all it's pretty authentic. Make this dish as your guests arrive—it should be eaten as soon as it's ready for the best results. If you have a fondue kit, simply pour the melted cheese into the fondue after it has been made. Make sure the fondue bowl has been prewarmed before adding the melted cheese mix.

2 shallots, or 1 white onion, finely chopped
2 teaspoons white wine vinegar
⅔ cup white wine
3¾ cups grated Gruyére cheese
3½ cups grated sharp cheddar cheese
1½ cups crumbled Gorgonzola cheese
1 tablespoon Dijon mustard or whole-grain mustard
heaping ¾ cup cream cheese
⅓ cup plus 1 tablespoon heavy cream
freshly ground black pepper

To serve
crusty bread (slightly stale) or croutons
cooked new potatoes (if you have leftover roast potatoes, these are great as well)
cornichon (mini gherkins or pickles)
pickled or raw cauliflower, carrots, baby turnips
salami or cured sausage, cut into chunky pieces
chunks of cooked ham

1 Place a large pot of water on the stove and bring to a boil. Place a bowl on top of the pan to create a bain-marie or water bath.

2 Put the chopped shallots or onion into a small saucepan with the vinegar and the white wine, bring to a boil, and continue to boil until reduced by half. Once reduced, pour the reduction into the bowl on top of the boiling water and add the Gruyére, cheddar, and blue cheese. Stir it around the pan slowly while the cheese melts. This will take around 15 minutes.

3 Once the cheese is nearly all melted, add the Dijon mustard, cream cheese, heavy cream, and lots of black pepper. Make sure all the ingredients are well combined and the cheeses melted.

4 If using a fondue kit, pour the mixture into the fondue bowl now. If you don't have a fondue kit, carefully take the bain-marie to the table and let everyone dig in with the prepared bits and pieces to be dipped.

If you feel like something a bit different, try adding a splash of truffle oil. You'll be guaranteed to get a few oohs and ahhs.

GREEN APPLE SLAW

15
TOTAL

Preparation 15
Cooking 0
Serves 6

Perfect with the Lamb Burgers and Chunky Potato Wedges (see page 123).

I love this dish, either crammed into a burger or on the side with some freshly barbecued seafood. It is the ultimate side dish that suits any alfresco or casual dining down to a tee.

For the dressing
1 tablespoon whole-grain mustard
2 lemons
⅔ cup crème fraîche or sour cream
salt and freshly ground black pepper

For the apple slaw
2 tablespoons plump golden raisins
4 tablespoons warm apple juice or water
¼ white cabbage, finely shredded
2 Spanish onions, peeled and finely sliced
4 Granny Smith apples
a large bunch of flatleaf parsley, chopped

1 Make the dressing for the slaw by combining all the ingredients in a bowl. Taste for seasoning. To plump up the raisins, let soak in a bowl containing the warm apple juice or water.

2 To make the slaw, put the cabbage in a large mixing bowl with the onions. Peel the apples and slice thinly to the core. Stack the slices and cut again to make very thin matchsticks. Add these to the cabbage and the onion. Then add the chopped parsley and soaked golden raisins.

3 Toss the slaw in the dressing and serve at room temperature.

AN EASY TART

30
TOTAL

Preparation 15

Cooking 15

Serves 4

as a main course or
6 to 8 as a light snack

**Puff pastry sheets
are great to keep
in the freezer for
any entertaining
emergencies and
also easy to pick
up from the chilled
section of your
grocery store.**

Puff pastry sheets are an ingredient that I couldn't do without. You can top them with anything you happen to have lying around and you've got a great little dinner. Store-bought pesto and tapenades are fantastic, baked in the oven with some mozzarella and then topped with basil leaves. I thought I'd go one step farther with this recipe—I love this salty combination.

1 sheet puff pastry measuring
   8 to 12 inches in length
1 portion chermoula (see page 48) or a jar
   of store-bought pesto
8 marinated anchovies, cut in half
   lengthwise

2 tablespoons capers
2 tablespoons black olives
7 ounces mozzarella cheese
2 tablespoons olive oil
1 egg, beaten
a small handful of basil leaves

1 Preheat the oven to 425°F. Lightly oil a large nonstick baking sheet. Lay out the puff pastry on the baking sheet. Score a border ¾ inch in from the edges of the pastry. This will allow the border to rise and crisp while the center stays flat.

2 Spread the chermoula over the inner section of the tart and crisscross the anchovies over the top. Scatter over the capers and olives and then tear over the mozzarella. Drizzle over the olive oil and brush the border with the beaten egg.

3 Bake in the oven for 10 to 15 minutes until the border rises and is golden brown. Remove from the oven and sprinkle with the basil leaves. Cut into pieces on a big board to put in the middle of the table so that everyone can help themselves.

DEEP-FRIED MOZZARELLA BALLS WITH JALAPEÑO CHEESE DIP

25

TOTAL

Preparation 15

Cooking 10

Serves 6

These are the ultimate friendly accompaniment to a cold beer or a classic frozen margarita (see page 172). I don't think any of your friends will be disappointed when served these spicy molten snacks.

For the sauce
heaping ¾ cup cream cheese
⅓ cup plus 1 tablespoon white wine or water
2 tablespoons chopped jalapeño chiles (from a jar)
4 to 5 splashes of Tabasco sauce
4 to 5 splashes of Worcestershire sauce
scant 1 cup grated cheddar cheese

For the mozzarella balls
heaping ¾ cup all-purpose flour
1½ cups dry bread crumbs
3 large eggs
1 quart vegetable oil, for deep-frying
30 bocconcini (tiny mozzarella balls)
salt

1 For the sauce, put the cream cheese in a saucepan with the wine or water on medium heat. Add the jalapeños and Tabasco and Worcestershire sauces. Gradually stir in the cheddar until it has melted. Keep warm while you make the mozzarella balls.

2 For the mozzarella balls, put the flour and bread crumbs in separate bowls and beat the eggs in a third. Pour the oil into a shallow, wide-based saucepan (don't fill it more than halfway) and put on medium heat.

3 Drain and pat the bocconcini dry. Coat first in the flour, then in the beaten egg, and finally in the bread crumbs. Then pass through the egg and bread crumbs once again to make sure they are coated really well.

4 Test the oil to see if it's hot enough by dropping in a pinch of bread crumbs. If they bubble and rise to the top, the oil is ready. Gently lower around six or eight balls at a time into the oil using a slotted spoon and deep-fry for about 1 minute until golden brown. Remove from the oil (again using the slotted spoon) and leave to drain on paper towels before sprinkling with salt.

5 Serve the mozzarella balls with the warm dip.

Perfect served with a few beers for friends or as an appetizer to the Mexican Beef Burritos (see page 139).

CRISPY FRIED SALT AND PEPPER SQUID WITH THAI DIPPING SAUCE

20
TOTAL

Preparation 15
Cooking 5
Serves 4
as an appetizer

Squid is really inexpensive and very easily sourced. Try to buy the baby ones with the tentacles tucked inside them, as they give a bit of interest to the dish. They are usually already cleaned, so all you have to do is heat up your oil and prepare the batter.

2 cups vegetable oil, for deep-frying
12 whole baby squid, cleaned
1 teaspoon baking powder
4 tablespoons all-purpose flour
2 tablespoons cornstarch
salt and freshly ground black pepper
about ½ cup sparkling water

For the Thai dipping sauce
1 tablespoon Thai fish sauce

1 teaspoon superfine sugar
juice of 2 limes
1 green pepper, chopped
2 scallions, trimmed and finely chopped

To serve
a small handful of cilantro, torn
1 lime, cut into wedges

1 Take a large heavy-bottomed saucepan and pour in the vegetable oil. Turn the heat to medium and let the oil heat up while you prepare the rest of the dish. If using a deep fryer, heat it to 340°F.

2 To prepare the squid, pull the tentacles out of the body. Cut off and discard the sack just above the start of the tentacles. Reserve the tentacles and cut the body into three strips. Dry all the pieces well on paper towels.

3 To make the batter, combine the baking powder, flour, cornstarch, salt, and pepper in a bowl and beat in the sparkling water. It should be the consistency of a thin yogurt.

4 To make the dipping sauce, combine the Thai fish sauce with the sugar and lime juice and mix well until the sugar has dissolved. Taste to check the balance—it should be not too sweet, nor too salty. Then add the chile and scallions.

5 Check that the oil is hot enough by dropping a pea-size drop of the batter into the oil. If it fizzles and bubbles, the oil is at the right temperature. Make sure you have paper towels and a slotted spoon to hand to remove the squid from the oil.

6 Coat the squid pieces in the batter and transfer to the hot oil with the slotted spoon, making sure you lay the squid away from you to avoid burns. Let the squid bubble until it is golden brown, 2 to 3 minutes. Remove from the oil, drain on paper towels, and serve straight away with the dip, some torn cilantro, and the lime wedges.

Serve as an appetizer with Sirloin Steak with Blue Cheese Butter (see page 88) or Shrimp and Egg Fried Rice (see page 46) to follow.

CORN AND SCALLION FRITTERS

30
TOTAL

Preparation 15
Cooking 15
Makes 12 to 15
small fritters

These are a great snack or side dish. They are very easy to cook and use ingredients that would generally be hanging around in your pantry or fridge. Dip them in guacamole or tomato salsa, or eat with sweet chili sauce.

8 tablespoons self-rising flour
1 teaspoon baking powder
salt and freshly ground black pepper
2 large eggs
1⅓ cups milk
2 x 7-ounce cans corn kernels, drained
3 scallions, trimmed and sliced

a small bunch of cilantro, coarsely
  chopped
1 red pepper, chopped
2 tablespoons vegetable oil
guacamole, tomato salsa, or sweet chili
  sauce, to serve (optional)

1 Mix the flour and baking powder in a bowl. Add the salt and pepper and make a well in the center of the flour. Crack the eggs into the well and beat together to form a paste. Gradually add the milk, continuously beating, until you have a batter with a thick dropping consistency.

2 Add the corn, scallions, cilantro, and chile to the batter. If it now looks a little thick, add a drop more milk. The batter needs to be able to hold its shape when poured into the pan to cook, so shouldn't be too thin.

3 Heat a skillet and add the vegetable oil. When the oil is hot, take a tablespoon of the mixture and drop it into the pan. Depending on the size of your pan you should be able to fit four fritters in at once. Cook until golden brown, 1½ minutes, and then flip them over. Cook for an additional 2 minutes on the other side and serve.

**Serve with the
Barbecue Chinese
Ribs (see page 118).**

MEXICAN BEEF BURRITOS WITH CHUNKY GUACAMOLE

45
TOTAL

Preparation 20

Cooking 25

Serves 4

or 6 as a light snack

Spicy Mexican is always great food to tuck into when you are socializing with friends. The dish is all self-assembled, so all you have to do is put the bowls in the middle of the table and let everyone dig in.

2 tablespoons vegetable oil
1 large red onion, peeled and finely chopped
2 to 3 hot red peppers, finely chopped (with the seeds in if you're brave enough)
4 garlic cloves, peeled and chopped
2 teaspoons ground cumin
1 teaspoon ground coriander
1¾ pounds lean ground beef
1 tablespoon tomato paste
salt and freshly ground black pepper
1 cup beef stock
1 x 14-ounce can whole plum tomatoes
a pinch of white sugar
1 x 14-ounce can red kidney beans, drained

For the guacamole
2 avocados
1 garlic clove, peeled and grated
1 red pepper, finely chopped
zest of 2 limes
½ bunch of cilantro, coarsely chopped
½ teaspoon ground cumin
1 tablespoon olive oil

To serve
tomato salsa
soft flour tortillas
sour cream
grated Monterey Jack, mozzarella, or cheddar cheese
sliced jalapeño peppers

1 To make the chile filling for the burritos, heat the oil in a large skillet or casserole dish. Add the onion, chiles, and garlic and sauté until softened, 5 to 6 minutes. Then add the cumin and coriander before increasing the heat and adding the ground beef. Try to get a little color on it, moving everything around in the pan to combine well.

2 Add the tomato paste, season with salt and pepper, and then add the stock, tomatoes, and sugar and cook for 15 to 20 minutes while you make the guacamole. Reduce the heat so the bottom won't burn and add the kidney beans. Add a bit of water if it looks like it's drying out too much, but be careful, as you don't want it sloppy.

3 To make the guacamole, cut the avocados in half, remove the pits, and scoop out the flesh using a spoon. Add the garlic, red pepper, and lime zest. Using the back of a fork, crush the avocado until you get a chunky purée. Then add the cilantro and ground cumin, season well, and add the olive oil. Stir and let stand until you are ready to serve. This can also be done in a blender if you prefer.

4 Serve the ground beef with warmed tortillas, the guacamole, salsa, sour cream, grated cheese, and some jalapeño chiles.

Have a look through the recipe before you start cooking. Most of the chopping can be done in one go. For example, all the chiles, garlic, and onions can be chopped at once to save you doing the job two or three times for different parts of the recipe.

CHICKEN, LEEK, AND BACON PIE

55
TOTAL

Preparation 15
Cooking 40
Serves 6

It's nice to make individual pies as in the picture opposite, but it works just as well making one large one.

A warm and homely pie, this one is perfect for the whole family but made in half the time of a usual pie, thanks to the ready-prepared puff pastry.

7 ounces smoked lardons or smoked bacon slices, chopped
18 ounces skinless, boneless chicken thighs, diced
2 bay leaves
salt and freshly ground black pepper

4 tablespoons butter
3 leeks, trimmed and sliced
3 tablespoons all-purpose flour
2 cups plus 1 tablespoon chicken stock
1 sheet puff pastry
1 egg, beaten

1 Preheat the oven to 400°F. Place a large saucepan on the stove on medium heat and add the lardons or chopped bacon. When this has started to crisp and go golden brown, add the chicken and bay leaves. Season with salt and pepper.

2 Add the butter and leeks to the pan, cover, and let the leeks cook until wilted, 3 to 5 minutes. Add the flour and stir well, then pour in the chicken stock. Stir well while the mixture comes to a boil. Remove from the heat and pour the mixture into a pie or casserole dish. Make sure you choose a dish or individual dishes that the puff pastry will cover. If using individual dishes, you may need 2 sheets of puff pastry.

3 Cut a strip of the puff pastry and mold the strip around the rim of the pie dish. Brush this with beaten egg and lay the remaining dough on top. Press down around the rim well and trim off any excess. Make a small hole in the top of the dough, brush well with beaten egg, and sprinkle with salt.

4 Bake the pie in the oven for about 30 minutes, or until the pastry is golden brown. Serve immediately.

Sweet Tooth

There are odd occasions when we all need a little sweet something. It might be a sneaky piece of chocolate or a big bowl of berries. Whatever your preferred sweet treats, it's always good to have a choice. In this chapter I have created simple desserts that can be cooked in minutes. No setting times or hours of baking involved. These dishes will only take a few minutes out of your busy day to make something comforting and sweet to finish off a meal perfectly. Some recipes may take a bit longer than others, but none are overly complicated. Whatever your dessert requirements are, I'm sure you will find something in here to satisfy yourself, friends, kids, and family.

BAKED APRICOT BRIOCHE

25
_____
TOTAL

Preparation 10
Cooking 15
Serves 6

**This dessert
works really
well with fresh
fruits such as
pears, peaches,
and nectarines,
especially when
ripe and in
season.**

This dish is a quick take on the much-loved bread and butter pudding, but without the cooking and setting time. It's no harder to prepare than making a quick sandwich.

**1 small brioche loaf or 3 large croissants
4 tablespoons softened unsalted butter
⅓ cup apricot jam**

**2 x 14-ounce cans apricot halves in juice
½ cup superfine sugar
vanilla ice cream or heavy cream, to serve**

1 Preheat the oven to 400°F. Slice the brioche loaf into six thick slices or the croissants in half lengthwise and butter on both sides. Lay the slices in an ovenproof dish measuring about 8 x 8 inches (you may need another brioche loaf to cover the bottom of the dish) and generously spread over the apricot jam.

2 Drain the apricots (reserving some of the juice) and lay, cut-side down, onto the buttered and jammed brioche. Sprinkle the sugar over the top and drizzle with 2 to 3 tablespoons of the reserved apricot juice.

3 Bake in the oven for 10 to 15 minutes until slightly crispy at the edges. Serve with the accompaniment of your choice.

ALMOND, HAZELNUT, AND VANILLA BUTTER COOKIES

20
TOTAL

Preparation 5
Cooking 15
Makes 12 to 14
cookies

You can freeze this dough in wax paper to have on standby.

If you don't feel like making a dessert when entertaining on a weeknight but feel you should satisfy that sweet tooth at the end of a meal, I have the perfect solution. Cookies served with a strong shot of espresso really hit the spot. Warm, freshly cooked cookies are a very special treat and a really elegant way to round off a meal.

⅔ cup unsalted butter
½ cup superfine sugar
¾ cup plus 1 tablespoon all-purpose flour

seeds scraped from ½ vanilla bean
heaping 1 cup ground almonds
½ cup lightly crushed hazelnuts

1 Preheat the oven to 350°F. Cream the butter and sugar together either in a blender or by hand until smooth and well combined. Fold in the flour, vanilla seeds, and almonds and combine well. Scatter in the hazelnuts.

2 Divide the mixture into 12 to 14 balls and place on a lined nonstick baking sheet, making sure they are not too close together. Bake in the oven for 15 minutes until golden brown. Let cool for a few minutes before serving. The cookies will keep for a week in an airtight container.

BERRY GRATIN

20

TOTAL

Preparation 15

Cooking 5

Serves 6

Don't worry about having matching ramekins for this. I always think it's quite nice to have a bit of mix and match.

This is such a lovely simple recipe and has a definite touch of class. Summery and colorful, it's a special way to finish off a meal.

1 cup heavy cream
1 teaspoon vanilla paste or 1 vanilla bean
4 eggs, separated
¾ cup superfine sugar
1 tablespoon cornstarch

splash of rum or Grand Marnier (optional)
18 ounces mixed summer berries, such as strawberries, blueberries, raspberries, and blackberries

1 Heat the cream in a saucepan on low heat with the vanilla paste or cut the vanilla bean in half lengthwise, scrape out the seeds with a small knife into the pan, and add the bean to infuse, too. Don't let it come to a boil.

2 In another saucepan, beat together the egg yolks, sugar, and cornstarch and slowly pour the hot cream over the mixture. Place the pan over low heat and stir continuously until the custard thickens to the consistency of thin yogurt, 5 to 6 minutes. Don't leave the custard on the stove without stirring or you will end up with scrambled eggs. Once thickened, remove from the heat. Add the splash of rum or Grand Marnier at this stage, if you wish.

3 Preheat the broiler to medium. Scatter the mixed berries in the bottom of either individual heatproof bowls or one large baking dish.

4 Beat the egg whites with a hand-held electric mixer until firm peaks start to form and carefully fold into the thickened custard. Pour the mixture over the berries and place under the broiler until an even golden brown, 1 to 2 minutes. Serve warm.

THE DREADED SOUFFLÉ (LEMON FLAVOR)

I can totally understand why people are so scared of soufflés. There are horror stories of them not rising, sinking, and exploding. My view is if you don't try, you'll never know. I've made imperfect soufflés in my time, but I'm not sure that anyone has ever really noticed at a dinner party. As long as they are light and fluffy, who cares what shape they are? This one is very easy, so please don't worry about it.

20
TOTAL

Preparation 10
Cooking 10
Serves 2

2 tablespoons unsalted butter
¼ cup superfine sugar, plus 2 teaspoons
2 large eggs, separated

2 tablespoons lemon curd
zest of 2 lemons
confectioners sugar, to serve

1 Preheat the oven to 400°F. Melt the butter in a small saucepan. Brush two small ramekins in an upward motion with the butter using a pastry brush. Put 1 teaspoon of sugar in each ramekin and roll it around so the inside is coated in sugar. Put them in the fridge.

2 Mix the egg yolks well with the lemon curd and the lemon zest in a large mixing bowl. In a separate clean and dry bowl, beat the whites using an electric mixer until stiff peaks start to form. Then, still beating, slowly start adding the sugar. When the whites are at firm peaks (so they stand on their own without flopping over), stop beating. Gently fold one large spoon of the whipped whites into the yolk and lemon curd mixture. Use a metal spoon to do this, then gradually add the rest until all the whites are folded into the yolks. Do this slowly and don't overwork the mixture.

3 Spoon the mixture into the buttered and sugared ramekins. Gently tap the ramekins on the work surface so that any bubbles rise to the top and smooth out the mixture with a spatula. Bake for about 10 minutes until well risen. Try not to open the door while they are cooking. Remove from the oven and sprinkle with confectioners sugar before serving immediately.

Try replacing the lemon curd with Nutella and a crushed ripe banana for a different twist.

AN EASY MESS

10

TOTAL

Preparation 10
Cooking 0
Serves 4

**You can use all
sorts of fruit for
this depending on
what's in season.
Stewed plums
with a pinch of
cinnamon work
particularly well.**

This is a classic recipe that never fails. However, the downside used to be that you would have had to wait three hours while you make the perfect crispy meringue, something that very few of us have time to do during the week while working. Thanks to our wonderfully stocked supermarkets, however, we cooks now have a solution... ready-made meringues. Now we can all make a mess with ease!

1 large ready-made meringue shell
scant 1 cup mascarpone cheese
⅔ cup confectioners sugar
½ cup crème fraîche or sour cream
1 vanilla bean, cut in half lengthwise and
   the seeds scraped out or 1 teaspoon
   vanilla bean paste
juice of ½ lemon

2 cups fresh strawberries
1⅔ cups fresh raspberries
4 scoops of vanilla or raspberry ripple
   ice cream

For the coulis
2½ cups fresh raspberries
1 tablespoon confectioners sugar

1 Put the meringue into a plastic bag and bash lightly using a rolling pin or similar heavy object.

2 Put the mascarpone in a bowl and stir well to loosen. Mix in the confectioners sugar together with the crème fraîche or sour cream, vanilla seeds or paste, and lemon juice. Hull the strawberries and cut into small pieces. Fold these through the sweetened cream together with the raspberries.

3 Make the coulis by pushing the raspberries though a fine strainer using the back of a spoon. Discard the seeds and sweeten the purée to taste with the confectioners sugar.

4 When you are ready to serve, fold the crushed meringues through the strawberry and raspberry cream. Put a scoop of your chosen ice cream in the bottom of your serving glass, drizzle with a little of the coulis, and pile on the cream. Drizzle with a final teaspoon of coulis before serving.

BLUEBERRY PIE

40

TOTAL

Preparation 10
Cooking 30
Serves 6

Serve after the
Sirloin Steak
with Blue
Cheese Butter
(see page 88).

Thanks to the convenient invention of ready-rolled pie crust, we no longer need to spend all our time crumbling, kneading, resting, and rolling the top for a lovely berry pie. The filling for this pie is simple and has great flavor, as the berries burst their juices when you bite into them. Accompanied by a crispy, sugary topping and cold ice cream, this pudding is the perfect way end to a meal.

juice of 2 lemons
6 tablespoons superfine sugar
scant ½ cup unsalted butter
1 tablespoon cornstarch
3⅓ cups blueberries
vanilla ice cream, to serve

For the pastry
1 sheet sweet pie crust
1 egg, beaten
a sprinkling of brown sugar
a pinch of ground cinnamon

1 Preheat the oven to 400°F. Make the filling by combining the lemon juice with the sugar in a small saucepan and heating gently. Add the butter and the cornstarch and mix to a smooth paste. Then add the blueberries and mix thoroughly.

2 Cut a thin strip off the edge of the sheet of pie crust and stick this around the edge of a 2-cup baking dish, using your thumb to press it to the rim. Pour the blueberries into the dish.

3 Paint the beaten egg around the pastry rim and lay over the remaining pie dough. Seal the edges using either your thumb or a fork and trim off any excess dough. Make a small hole in the top for steam to escape and paint more egg wash over the top. Sprinkle with the sugar and cinnamon and bake in the oven for about 30 minutes until the top is golden brown and crisp.

4 Serve with vanilla ice cream.

CHOCOLATE AND ORANGE YORKIES

20–22
TOTAL

Preparation 10
Cooking 10–12
Serves 6

Try using white chocolate and raspberries for an alternative.

This is a sweet variation on the English savory dish Yorkshire pudding, traditionally served with roast beef. In fact, it's not a pudding at all but a simple batter mix, to which I have added sugar. Of course, I have also added a few other ingredients to make it even more inviting and tempting... that's my job. Just make sure you serve this sweet version after the main meal instead of with the roast!

6 teaspoons vegetable oil
1¾ cups plus 1 tablespoon all-purpose flour
3 tablespoons superfine sugar
1 teaspoon baking powder
zest of 2 oranges

3 eggs, lightly beaten
1 cup lowfat milk
½ teaspoon vanilla extract
about ⅔ cup chocolate buttons
heavy cream, to serve

1 Preheat the oven to 425°F. Pour half a teaspoon of vegetable oil into each cup of a 12-cup muffin pan and place in the oven to heat up.

2 Put the flour into a bowl with the sugar, baking powder, and orange zest. Make a well in the center of the flour and pour in the eggs. Beat together with a hand-held electric mixer before slowly adding the milk and then mix in the vanilla extract.

3 Remove the muffin pan carefully from the oven and pour an equal amount of the batter into each one. Drop 4 to 5 chocolate buttons into each muffin cup and bake for 10 to 12 minutes until risen and golden brown. Serve while hot with heavy cream.

BANANA PUDDING WITH TOFFEE SAUCE

20
TOTAL

Preparation 10
Cooking 10
Serves 4 to 6

If you're really
pushed for time,
serve with vanilla
ice cream instead.

I love the word pudding, although I'm not entirely sure what it means. Whatever it is, this particular recipe just about sums up the word to me and I promise, even if people say they don't want dessert, they will when you bring this one out and put it on the table. You don't even have to get more than one bowl dirty. A fork, wooden spoon, and a baking dish is all you need for the pudding, plus a saucepan for the sauce. How much easier can you get?

**scant ½ cup softened unsalted butter, plus
  extra for greasing**
3 ripe bananas
¾ cup plus 1 tablespoon all-purpose flour
1 teaspoon baking powder
1 teaspoon ground cinnamon
½ cup light brown sugar
a pinch of salt

1 teaspoon vanilla paste or extract
2 eggs, beaten
2 tablespoons milk

For the toffee sauce
heaping ⅓ cup light brown sugar
⅓ cup butter
⅓ cup plus 1 tablespoon heavy cream

1 Grease a 1-quart baking dish (make sure it fits in your microwave) with butter. Add the remaining butter to the dish and microwave on medium for 30 seconds until it has melted. Keep your eye on it, as you don't want it to explode and make a mess.

2 Peel two of the bananas and crush them into the melted butter using the back of a fork. Add the flour, baking powder, cinnamon, sugar, salt, and vanilla and mix well with a wooden spoon. Then add the eggs and milk and combine to form a paste. Gently tap the dish on the work surface to even out the mixture and slice the remaining banana on top. Cover with plastic wrap and put in the microwave. Cook on high heat for 8 minutes.

3 Meanwhile, make the toffee sauce by boiling the sugar and butter in a saucepan for 3 to 4 minutes, then add the cream. Allow the sauce to bubble and then serve with the banana pudding.

PINEAPPLE SKEWERS WITH VANILLA AND MAPLE SYRUP

20

TOTAL

Preparation 10
Cooking 10
Serves 4 to 6

This is great cooked
on the barbecue if
the weather is nice.

This is a really straightforward dessert and hot pineapple with cold ice cream and sweet syrup is something very special. This recipe is also great with banana.

1 supersweet medium-size pineapple or 2 to 3 containers of pineapple, precut into chunks

1 teaspoon vanilla paste or 1 vanilla bean
6 tablespoons maple syrup
vanilla ice cream, to serve

1 Preheat a grill pan or large skillet on medium heat. If you have bought a whole fresh pineapple, you will need to top and tail it. Remove the spiky outer skin using a serrated knife, trying to remove the eyes (brown spots) on the flesh as you go. Cut the pineapple in half, and then cut each half into four or five strips. Remove the middle woody core. Push the pineapple strip onto wooden or metal skewers. If you have bought precut pineapple, it will be in chunks, so push five to six onto each skewer.

2 In a saucepan, mix the vanilla paste or seeds (removed from the bean using a small knife) with the maple syrup and gently heat to a simmer. Brush the syrup onto the pineapple skewers. Lay onto the hot grill pan and cook until they start to caramelize. Turn in the pan to ensure they cook and color evenly. Brush with the syrup as you go. This can also be done under the broiler, but you must soak the skewers if you are using wooden ones or they will burn.

3 Remove from the pan, pour over the remaining syrup, and serve with ice cream.

PEACH AND PISTACHIO TRIFLE

15

TOTAL

Preparation 15
Cooking 0
Serves 6

It's really important to keep your pantry stocked up with the basics and canned peaches, apricots, and pears are all useful essentials. When not in season, these canned fruits have a great texture, flavor, and sweetness to liven up a quick dessert.

¾ cup plus 1 tablespoon heavy cream
scant 1 cup mascarpone cheese
zest and juice of 1 large orange
½ teaspoon vanilla extract or paste
1 cup confectioners sugar
2 x 14-ounce cans peach halves in juice
2 tablespoons Madeira wine or sweet
   sherry

½ brioche loaf or 1 loaf Madeira cake,
   cut into ½-inch thick slices
1 cup pistachio nuts in shell, shelled and
   skinned if possible, coarsely chopped
a small handful of mint leaves
2 tablespoons honey

1 Whip the cream in a large bowl until soft peaks form. In a separate bowl, beat the mascarpone and fold it into the cream. Add the orange zest and juice and vanilla extract or paste and sift in the confectioners sugar. Stir to mix.

2 Drain the peaches and reserve the juice. Pour the juice into a bowl and add the Madeira or sweet sherry. Add 2 tablespoons of the sherry-flavored peach juice to the cream mixture and beat well.

3 Slice by slice, dip the brioche or Madeira cake into the flavored peach juice, just long enough to coat the cake but not allowing it to go soggy. Lay each slice in the bottom of a serving dish until all the gaps are filled on the bottom.

4 Lay the drained peaches on top of the cake and then generously spoon over the sweetened cream up to the rim of the dish. Sprinkle with the chopped pistachios, tear over the mint leaves, and drizzle with the honey. Serve immediately.

Skinned pistachios are available from most Turkish markets if you have difficulty finding them elsewhere.

RICOTTA AND RASPBERRY FRITTERS WITH CINNAMON

20–25
TOTAL

Preparation 10
Cooking 10–15
Serves 6

Oh so easy to prepare and far too easy to eat! A great dessert for finger food at the end of a big dinner party. You must try these—trust me, you'll wish you made more of the batter, once the first batch has been devoured.

about 2 cups vegetable oil, for deep-frying
1 cup ricotta
1 egg
2 egg yolks
6 tablespoons all-purpose flour

2 level teaspoons baking powder
1½ teaspoons ground cinnamon
5 tablespoons superfine sugar
1¼ cups fresh raspberries

1 Pour enough oil into a wide, deep skillet so that it's about 2 inches deep but not more than halfway full. Heat the oil to 340°F on medium heat. If you have a deep fryer, heat it to 340°F.

2 Put the ricotta into a bowl and add the egg, egg yolks, flour, baking powder, ½ teaspoon of the cinnamon, and 2 tablespoons of the sugar. Using a hand-held electric mixer, beat the mixture until smooth. Gently fold in the raspberries. Mix the remaining sugar and cinnamon together in a shallow dish and set aside for later.

3 Check to see if the oil is at the right temperature by dropping in a pea-size drop of the batter. If it sizzles in the oil, you know it's hot enough. Get ready to deep-fry by making sure you have a slotted spoon and paper towels to drain the oil off the fritters once cooked.

4 Using a tablespoon, take a spoonful of the mixture (try to get one raspberry per spoonful) and drop it carefully into the hot oil. Use another spoon to push the mixture off the spoon if you need to. Don't put too many into the pan at once. Deep-fry each fritter until golden brown, about 3 to 4 minutes, turning once or twice in the oil to make sure the color is even. They will puff up and expand while cooking.

5 Remove the cooked fritters from the oil with a slotted spoon and place on paper towels to drain. Once all the fritters are cooked, roll them in the sugar and cinnamon mix and serve immediately while still hot.

Turn off the oil and let it cool completely before discarding.

TIRAMISU

15
TOTAL

Preparation 15
Cooking 0
Makes 4
large, 6 small

You can make this in advance, as it will keep for a few days in the fridge. Just re-dust with cocoa before you serve.

This is still one of my all-time favorite desserts and it's so easy to prepare. I make this at nearly every dinner party and I'm sure my guests are getting bored of it by now, but I just can't help it.

3 eggs, separated
1 teaspoon vanilla paste or extract
8 tablespoons confectioners sugar
zest of 1 lemon
1 shot Madeira wine (or any fortified wine)

2¼ cups mascarpone cheese
16 Amaretti cookies
3 tablespoons espresso or very
 strong coffee
unsweetened cocoa, to serve

1 Beat the egg yolks together with the vanilla paste, confectioners sugar, lemon zest, and Madeira with a hand-held electric mixer until pale. When pale, add the mascarpone cheese and beat again.

2 In a separate clean and dry bowl, whip the whites using the electric mixer (with cleaned beaters) until stiff peaks start to form. Fold into the mascarpone mixture.

3 Soak the Amaretti cookies in the coffee and lay two in the bottom of each serving glass. Spoon a generous amount of mascarpone cream on top of each one and dust with cocoa. Soak the remaining cookies in the coffee and put on top of the mascarpone cream. Evenly distribute the remaining cream and smooth over the top. Dust with cocoa as you are about to serve.

VANILLA RICE PUDDING WITH BLUEBERRY COMPOTE

25
___
TOTAL

Preparation 5
Cooking 20
Serves 6 to 8

**Use a spoonful
or two of your
favorite jam
instead of a fruit
compote for a
quick cheat.**

I love rice pudding but I really don't like it when it's baked in the oven. So I always cook rice pudding as I would a risotto and serve it with something fruity—blueberries, in this case, but rhubarb, raspberry, strawberry, or peach will also do nicely.

3 cups plus 2 tablespoons lowfat milk
1 teaspoon vanilla paste or vanilla bean,
  split in half lengthwise
heaping ¾ cup superfine sugar
1½ cups short-grain or risotto rice
⅓ cup plus 1 tablespoon heavy cream

For the compote
2¾ cups fresh or frozen blueberries
zest and juice of 1 large orange
4 tablespoons superfine sugar
a pinch of ground cinnamon
2 tablespoons unsalted butter

1 Pour the milk into a saucepan and add the vanilla paste or vanilla bean and the sugar. Add the rice and bring to a boil. Reduce the heat and let the rice simmer. Stir every 2 to 3 minutes until the rice is cooked.

2 Meanwhile, make the blueberry compote. Put the blueberries into a saucepan (if using frozen there is no need to thaw them first) and add the orange zest and juice, sugar, cinnamon, and butter with 2 tablespoons of water. Cook on low heat until soft, about 10 minutes.

3 Once the rice is cooked and the milk absorbed, pour in the cream and pull out the vanilla bean. Heat through again, spoon the pudding into bowls, and serve with a spoonful of the compote.

Fancy a Drink?

If I am entertaining or celebrating a special occasion, cocktails are always on the must list. A few of the recipes in this book have been created to make your life while entertaining that little bit easier and that should not stop with food. Cocktails always make a party or any social event go with a swing, but making them can often be quite time-consuming. I want to show you my cheat sheets of getting around all that Boston shaking and muddling of the mojitos. All these drinks can sit happily in a pitcher in the fridge and then be finished over crushed ice or with a splash of something fizzy.

PEACH BELLINI

5

TOTAL

Preparation 5

Makes 10 to 12

cocktails

Peach purée is available in most grocery stores in the drinks section or in the desserts section.

This is a bit of a cheat, but I find that it's the best Bellini. It's easy to make and perfect for a busy party.

1 x 14-ounce can peaches or ¾ cup plus 1 tablespoon peach purée

⅓ cup plus 1 tablespoon vodka
2 bottles Prosecco, to serve

1 Put the canned peaches with their syrup and the vodka into a food processor. Blend to a purée and then keep in a pitcher or squeeze bottle until ready to serve. If using peach purée, mix the purée with the vodka and set aside.

2 When ready, put a small amount of the peach purée at the bottom of a champagne glass. Tilt the glass very slightly and pour the Prosecco down the side of the glass, trying to create a layer. You can also pour it down the back of a teaspoon. Serve while the bubbles are still fizzing and add a stirrer for presentation if you wish.

A CLASSIC COSMO

5

TOTAL

Preparation 5

plus chilling time

Makes 8 to 10

martini-size glasses

This is the best cocktail to put in the freezer and let chill. It saves shaking it over ice every time you get another request from a guest and—trust me—you will.

1¾ cups plus 2 tablespoons vodka
1¼ cups cranberry juice
⅔ cup Cointreau

5 tablespoons fresh lime juice
strips of orange zest, to serve

Mix all the ingredients in a large pitcher. Chill in the freezer and then, once it is really ice cold, transfer to the fridge.

CHILE AND GINGER MOJITO

10
TOTAL

Preparation 10

Makes 8

cocktails

This is a mojito that is guaranteed to give a little kick. You don't want to make it so spicy that it blows your head off, you just want a little twinge at the back of your throat that tells you you've just had chile. The ginger freshens the drink up really nicely and goes so well with the classic minty rum-based cocktail.

3 large red chiles, seeded and cut into fine strips
4-inch piece of fresh ginger, peeled and cut into fine strips
10 brown sugar cubes
6 limes, cut into eighths

2 large handfuls of mint leaves
crushed ice
8 tablespoons simple syrup (sugar syrup)
2 cups plus 1 tablespoon golden spiced rum
1⅔ cups apple juice (optional)

1 Put the chile and ginger in a bowl with the sugar, lime, and mint. Using the end of a rolling pin, crush all the ingredients together well. (You can also do this with a mortar and pestle.) Let stand covered in the fridge until the party starts.

2 When your guests arrive, spoon out a tablespoon of the mint and lime mix into each glass and add the crushed ice. Add 1 tablespoon of simple syrup to each cocktail and mix this around before topping up with golden rum. I usually add a splash of apple juice to sweeten it up a bit (and make it a bit less lethal).

RUM PUNCH

5
TOTAL

Preparation 5

plus chilling time

Makes 12

cocktails

I learned this cocktail while working in Tobago last year. My clients loved a pitcher of this delicious drink before heading out for the night, and I must say that I became rather partial to a small glass myself. It's fruity and fresh, not to mention dangerous, as you don't realize just how strong it is.

⅓ cup plus 1 tablespoon fresh lime juice
¾ cup plus 1 tablespoon grenadine syrup
1¼ cups golden rum

¾ cup plus 1 tablespoon pineapple juice
¾ cup plus 1 tablespoon grapefruit juice
10 splashes Angostura bitters

Mix in a large pitcher or individual glasses, chill, and serve with ice!

THE TOM PEPPER

5

TOTAL

Preparation 5
plus chilling time

Makes 8
cocktails

Oh no, egos are going to grow! Huge thanks to Jason Capper for the recipe and to Tom ... for everything!

1⅔ cups vodka
¾ cup plus 1 tablespoon puréed
   strawberries
½ cup berry liqueur
½ cup lemon juice

¾ cup plus 1 tablespoon sparkling wine

To serve
sliced strawberries
cracked black pepper

1 Mix all the ingredients in a pitcher and chill in the fridge until needed.

2 When ready to serve, pour over crushed ice in individual glasses and top with sparkling wine. Finish with strawberry slices and cracked black pepper.

A CLASSIC MARGARITA

5

TOTAL

Preparation 5
plus chilling time

Makes 10 to 12
cocktails

It's impossible to eat Mexican food with friends without a pitcher of frozen margaritas. I know you are meant to roll the edge of the glass in salt, but I'm not such a fan of this so I do fifty/fifty—half sugar, half salt. It's sensible to go for a good tequila, or you'll feel it the next day.

1¼ quarts tequila
2½ cups Cointreau
1¼ cups fresh lime juice
crushed ice

3 tablespoons salt
3 tablespoons superfine sugar
1 lime, cut into 8 slices, to garnish

1 To prepare the cocktail in advance, mix the tequila, Cointreau, and lime juice together and let stand in the fridge. This can be drunk as it is, but I like mine frozen.

2 When you're ready to serve, put the ice into a blender and add the margarita mixture. Mix the salt and sugar in a bowl and rub lime juice around the rim of each glass. Dip the glasses into the salt and sugar mixture, pour out the frozen margaritas, and serve.

30
MINUTE MEALS INDEX

30–60
MINUTE MEALS INDEX

INGREDIENTS INDEX